KING LEAR: A GUIDE

The Shakespeare Handbooks

KING LEAR

A Guide

ALISTAIR McCALLUM

Ivan R. Dee

CHICAGO

Library of Congress Cataloging-in-Publication Data:
McCallum, Alistair, 1954–
    King Lear : a guide / Alistair McCallum.
      p.   cm. —— (The Shakespeare handbooks)
    ISBN 1-56663-362-1 (cloth : alk. paper) —— ISBN 1-56663-363-X (pbk. : alk. paper)
    1. Shakespeare, William, 1564–1616. King Lear—Handbooks, manuals, etc.
    2. Lear, King (Legendary character), in literature—Handbooks, manuals, etc.
    I. Title.

PR2819 .M38 2001
822.3'3—dc21   00-066031

Introduction

In many ways, the plays of Shakespeare's time had a great deal in common with the movie scripts of today. Their prime purpose was to entertain. They were often written to tight deadlines and frequently involved collaboration between writers. Constant revision, cutting and rewriting were the norm. Considerations such as the available actors, current political events, and the changing tastes of the public always had to be borne in mind. Particular productions might excite interest and controversy, but plays were regarded as ephemeral and were rarely published in book form. The poet or essayist might produce a slim, finely bound volume in the hope of literary immortality, but the playwright worked and lived firmly in the present. Plays had not yet become literature. Theatregoing was a pleasure, not a duty.

Four hundred years later, a great deal has changed. Shakespeare is no longer simply a popular playwright; he has become a symbol, an icon. His name generates enthusiasm and anxiety in equal measure. Competing armies of literary critics - a profession unknown in Shakespeare's day - are engaged in a ceaseless war over his reputation and the meaning of his work.

I was lucky enough to grow up in Stratford-on-Avon and, as a regular visitor to the Royal Shakespeare Theatre, became familiar with many of the plays. Whatever else Shakespeare might be, he was not intimidating. The mist surrounding the plays gradually cleared; structure, characters, and ideas started to emerge; the creative input of actors, directors and crew became apparent. The better I understood the plays, the more absorbing and meaningful they became. Familiarity certainly did not breed contempt.

Without this degree of familiarity, approaching a Shakespeare play can be a daunting business. Where do we look for help? There is certainly no shortage of excellent books that discuss, interpret, and analyze Shakespeare's work. But for most of us the problems in approaching Shakespeare are essentially practical: the complexity of his plots, compounded by the obscurity (to modern ears) of his language. What was entirely missing, it seemed to me, was something to guide readers through these difficulties and give them the confidence to respond freely to the plays. This is what I have attempted to provide with the *Shakespeare Handbooks*. Each book gives a straightforward, detailed account of the plot, scene by scene, with plenty of quotations from the play itself, and help with the more obscure words and phrases. I have also included a handful of comments from writers of diverse periods, backgrounds, and opinions, which I hope readers will find thought-provoking, and a few pertinent facts and figures relating to Shakespeare's life and times.

Of course there is no single correct interpretation of a Shakespeare play. His plays were scripts, after all, for his own acting company, a close-knit group of men who worked together for many years; he wrote no introductions or footnotes, and precious few stage directions. The scenery and costumes, the movements and interactions of characters, the mood of the play—all these aspects, and many more, will always be matters for the imaginative judgment of those staging the play. And above all, the creative responses of spectators and readers will be many, varied, and unpredictable.

Shakespeare is challenging. His plays are rich, profound, and enigmatic. The experience of staging, performing, watching or reading them should be a journey of exploration. I hope that the *Shakespeare Handbooks* will give my readers help and encouragement with the first few steps of that rewarding journey.

KING LEAR: A GUIDE

Setting the scene

Shakespeare wrote *King Lear* in or around 1605. He was in his early forties, at the peak of his creative powers, and had established a formidable reputation. He was principal playwright for the King's Men, widely regarded as the best theatre company in England.

The basic story that Shakespeare used for *King Lear* - that of an old king who gives away his kingdom to his three daughters - was a well-known folk tale of the time, with roots in both history and mythology. It is possible that Shakespeare had acted in a play based on the same story - *The True Chronicle History of King Leir* - many years before. The author of this earlier work is not known. Shakespeare, as always, adapted and transformed his source materials, creating from the old legend a tragic masterpiece of astonishing power and intensity.

King Lear is set in the distant past, centuries before the birth of Christ. The world of the play is bleak and uncompromising; its characters are forced to make difficult choices, to confront burning questions, and to try to make sense of their universe. In response to suffering, malice and injustice, they appeal frequently to nature, but nature is indifferent; they call on the gods, but the gods are silent. In *King Lear*, human beings are, inescapably, responsible for their own fate. In the course of the play, this responsibility becomes painfully clear. There is a gradual movement towards self-knowledge, a realisation of people's dependence on one another, and an appreciation of the importance of honesty and compassion. But this understanding is gained at a terrible cost.

The language of *King Lear* is dense, difficult and impatient. It is bursting with references to the animal kingdom, to raw nature, and to physical cruelty. Concepts of justice, society, duty and loyalty are dissected mercilessly, and amid all this richness of language and thought the word 'nothing' echoes sombrely throughout the play.

"It is an immense play, immense in power and meaning and in the weight of tragic knowledge which it conveys. Both poetically and dramatically it goes as far as poetic drama can go."

David Daiches, *A Critical History of English Literature*, 1960

The division of the kingdom

Lear, King of Britain, is growing old.

He intends to divide his kingdom between his three daughters, Goneril, Regan and Cordelia. The daughters, along with their respective husbands, will each govern a third of the kingdom: Lear will remain King in title only.

Goneril is married to the Duke of Albany, and Regan to the Duke of Cornwall. Lear's youngest daughter, Cordelia, is unmarried; two suitors, the Duke of Burgundy and the King of France, are now in Lear's court.

CURTAIN UP

An open secret

I, i

Two of Lear's councillors, the Earls of Gloucester and Kent, are discussing the division of the kingdom. Although they had expected the King to show a degree of favouritism one way or another, it now appears that Lear has been scrupulous in making each portion of the kingdom - or at least the two portions destined for his married daughters - equal in size and value.

Gloucester introduces Kent to his son, Edmund, who has been abroad for nine years. Edmund is an illegitimate son, but Gloucester is no longer embarrassed to admit the fact. If anything, Edmund's birth outside wedlock is a source of amusement rather than shame:

Gloucester	. . . I have so often blush'd to acknowledge him, that now I am braz'd[1] to't.
Kent	I cannot conceive you.
Gloucester	Sir, this young fellow's mother could; whereupon she grew round-womb'd, and had, indeed, Sir, a son for her cradle ere she had a husband for her bed.

[1] *brazened, hardened*

Gloucester also has a legitimate son, Edgar, who is a year or so older than his illegitimate brother. Gloucester is equally fond of both sons, he assures Kent, mentioning that Edmund is due to go abroad again shortly.

Lear's ceremony comes to grief

King Lear enters with his daughters, sons-in-law and attendants. He sends Gloucester out to bring in Cordelia's suitors, the King of France and the Duke of Burgundy: as well as Lear's public announcement of the division of the kingdom, this is to be the occasion on which Cordelia declares her choice of husband.

Lear then solemnly proclaims that he is relinquishing the government of the kingdom:

Lear   . . . 'tis our fast[1] intent
To shake all cares and business from our age,
Conferring them on younger strengths, while
         we
Unburthen'd crawl toward death.

   [1] *fixed, unalterable*

However, before making the final allocation of the three portions of land, Lear presents his daughters with a challenge. He wants each one to make a public declaration of her love for her father: although he has already decided in his own mind on the boundaries of the three portions, and who is to receive each one, he hints that the daughter who can convince him that she loves him the most will be treated more generously than her sisters.

Goneril, Lear's eldest daughter, is asked to speak first. She promptly makes a short, polished speech in which she declares her boundless love for her father:

Goneril   Sir, I love you more than word can wield the
                  matter;
              Dearer than eye-sight, space and liberty;
              Beyond what can be valued rich or rare;
              No less than life, with grace, health, beauty,
                  honour;
              As much as child e'er lov'd . . .

The speech is patently insincere, but it delights Lear. He shows her, on the map of Britain, the territory that will from now on belong to her and her husband Albany, and to their heirs, in perpetuity. He then calls on Regan to declare her love. Regan too produces a false, glib speech and Lear, gratified again, presents the third of the kingdom that will be ruled by her and her husband Cornwall.

It is now the turn of Cordelia, Lear's youngest daughter. She has been observing the proceedings with distaste, uncomfortable with her father's desire for flattery and her sisters' complicity. She does not wish to be a part of this display, and says so bluntly:

Lear	Now, our joy,
	Although our last, and least;[1] to whose young love
	The vines of France and milk of Burgundy
	Strive to be interess'd;[2] what can you say to draw
	A third more opulent than your sisters? Speak.
Cordelia	Nothing, my lord.
Lear	Nothing?
Cordelia	Nothing.
Lear	Nothing will come of nothing: speak again.
Cordelia	Unhappy that I am, I cannot heave
	My heart into my mouth . . .

[1] *youngest and smallest*
[2] *connected: joined by marriage*

Lear is displeased. Cordelia persists: she loves him as a daughter should love her father, not with the overwhelming passion that Goneril and Regan claim to feel. If their love for their father dominates their lives so completely, she asks, why did they marry? For her part, she intends to find room in her heart for a husband as well as a father.

Lear gives Cordelia one final chance to follow her sisters' example. She refuses. He erupts in rage, and on a furious impulse disowns her utterly:

Lear	So young, and so untender?
Cordelia	So young, my Lord, and true.
Lear	Let it be so; thy truth then be thy dower:[1]
	For, by the sacred radiance of the sun,
	The mysteries of Hecate[2] and the night,
	By all the operation of the orbs[3]
	From whom we do exist and cease to be,
	Here I disclaim all my paternal care . . .

[1] *dowry*
[2] *goddess of the underworld*
[3] *spheres within which the stars and planets move*

Nothing, my lord.

"The whole titanic drama turns on this 'Nothing' and the bizarre fact that Cordelia's true love cannot find words to declare itself. And it is whirled on this axis by the fact that the treacherous, loveless ones possess an inexhaustible wealth of plausible language."

Ted Hughes, *Shakespeare and the Goddess of Complete Being*, 1992

Kent intervenes

The Earl of Kent tries to interrupt, but Lear refuses to give way. What angers him most is that the young Cordelia had been his favourite daughter, and he had looked forward to spending his last years with her:

Lear   I lov'd her most, and thought to set my rest[1]
On her kind nursery.[2]

> [1] *stake everything; rely completely*
> [2] *tender care*

The third of the kingdom that was destined for Cordelia is now to be divided between the other two sisters. All Lear's land, wealth and power is thus to be transferred to Goneril and Regan and their husbands. Lear announces that he will retain the title of King and, escorted by a company of a hundred knights, intends to live with his two daughters, spending a month in the household of each in turn. He hands the coronet which was to be Cordelia's on her marriage - symbolising her rule over a third of Britain - to Albany and Cornwall.

Kent interrupts again. Although he knows he is risking his life by publicly disagreeing with the King, he urges Lear to think again. Cordelia's love is deep and genuine, he insists, and it is an act of folly to dispossess her and give everything to her sisters, who may be more articulate but are certainly less sincere.

Furious at Kent's insolence, Lear draws his sword, and is on the verge of executing him on the spot, but the intervention of Albany and Cornwall saves him. Kent is unrepentant. He has been a loyal servant to Lear for many years and, he insists, his intention is to make the King see reason, for his own good. Lear solemnly declares that Kent, for his arrogance in contradicting him, is banished:

Lear   Five days we do allot thee for provision
To shield thee from disasters of the world;
And on the sixth to turn thy hated back
Upon our kingdom: if on the tenth day
    following
Thy banish'd trunk be found in our dominions,

> The moment is thy death. Away! By Jupiter,
> This shall not be revok'd.

Kent bids a fond farewell to Cordelia, reassuring her that she is in the right. To Goneril and Regan he expresses the cynical hope that their treatment of their father may live up to their fine words. With the consolation that he is escaping the madness that suddenly seems to have engulfed Lear and his court, he takes his leave.

Cordelia's suitors make their decisions

Gloucester now returns, accompanied by the King of France and the Duke of Burgundy. The three men are unaware of the angry scenes that have just taken place.

Lear addresses Burgundy first. He asks him, directly, what he expects to receive as Cordelia's dowry if he should marry her. Burgundy, hoping to come into possession of a third of the kingdom, is thrown into confusion. Maintaining a formal, diplomatic manner, he states that he assumes Lear's original offer to be unchanged. When he learns that Cordelia has been disowned, and will have no dowry whatsoever, Burgundy is lost for words; he cannot publicly admit his disappointment, but on the other hand he does not wish to suggest that he is still interested in Cordelia. He says, politely but evasively, that it is impossible to make a decision in the circumstances.

Lear now turns to the King of France. He will not insult the great King, he says, by offering him the hand of the worthless Cordelia. France, more open and frank than his rival Burgundy, is curious to know how Cordelia has so suddenly fallen out of favour. He cannot believe her capable of doing anything terrible enough to warrant her punishment. At this point

Cordelia speaks up in her own defence, and France immediately understands the nature of what has happened:

Cordelia	. . . It is no vicious blot, murther or foulness,
	No unchaste action, or dishonour'd step,
	That hath depriv'd me of your grace and favour,
	But even for want[1] of that for which I am
	richer,
	A still-soliciting eye,[2] and such a tongue
	That I am glad I have not, though not to have
	it
	Hath lost me in your liking.
Lear	Better thou
	Hadst not been born than not t'have pleased me
	better.
France	Is it but this? a tardiness[3] in nature
	Which often leaves the history unspoke
	That it intends to do?

[1] *lack*

[2] *an eye that is continually looking out for opportunities and advantages*

[3] *reticence, reserve*

France also realises that Burgundy's interest in Cordelia has been for her dowry, not herself. He prompts his rival to commit himself one way or the other: Burgundy replies that he will gladly marry Cordelia on the terms originally agreed, but cannot accept her now that she has displeased her father.

France finds that his feelings for Cordelia, rejected for her simple honesty, are now stronger than ever, and he immediately asks for her hand in marriage:

France   Fairest Cordelia, that art most rich, being poor;
Most choice, forsaken; and most lov'd, despis'd!
Thee and thy virtues here I seize upon . . .
Thy dowerless daughter, King, thrown to my
    chance,
Is Queen of us, of ours, and our fair France:
Not all the dukes of wat'rish[1] Burgundy
Can buy this unpriz'd precious maid of me.
Bid them farewell, Cordelia, though unkind:
Thou losest here, a better where to find.

[1] *of the country, rich in rivers and streams: of the
man, weak and unemotional*

Lear, scornful of France's decision, tells him that he is free to marry her; she is no longer his daughter. He refuses to say a single word of good will to France or Cordelia, and never wishes to see either of them again. He makes an angry exit, followed by his sons-in-law, attendants and the unlucky Burgundy.

> *"Cordelia simply resists Lear's claim to be the sun around which everything revolves. The mere presence of another inviolable person is enough to shatter Lear's identity."*
>
> Linda Bamber, *The Woman Reader in King Lear*, 1986

King Lear's request to his daughters to declare their love publicly is generally regarded as an act of vanity and folly. However, it is possible to interpret the scene in an entirely different way.

Lear had been planning to live with Cordelia, the daughter whom he loved (and perhaps trusted) the most. There is the suggestion that her third of the kingdom was richer than those of her sisters: could it be that his ultimate intention was for her to succeed to the throne on his death? If so, it was essential to forestall the objections of Goneril and Regan:

"His shrewd knowledge of his elder daughters put them in a position in which it would have been ludicrous for them to repudiate their father's judgement after their fulsome speeches of devotion . . . the love-test, taking them by surprise, trapped them into professions which they otherwise might never have made."

Harry V. Jaffa, *The Limits of Politics*, 1957

Cordelia foresees trouble

Cordelia now takes her leave of her sisters. She is deeply concerned about her father's welfare, which will now be in their hands:

Cordelia   The jewels of our father, with wash'd eyes
Cordelia leaves you: I know you what you are;
And like a sister am most loth to call
Your faults as they are named. Love well our
father:
To your professed bosoms[1] I commit him:
But yet, alas! stood I within his grace,
I would prefer him to a better place.

[1] *the love that you claim to feel*

Regan and Goneril respond sharply: Cordelia should mind her own business and be thankful that, impoverished as she now is, she has a husband to provide for her.

Apprehensive about the future, but powerless to do anything, Cordelia sets off with her husband for a new life in France.

Lear's future is discussed

Regan and Goneril, now alone, broach the subject of their father's behaviour. They quickly establish that they are of the same mind. Lear has always been unstable and temperamental, they agree, and in his old age is likely to become more so:

Goneril	. . . he always lov'd our sister most; and with what poor judgment he hath now cast her off appears too grossly.[1]
Regan	'Tis the infirmity of his age; yet he hath ever but slenderly known himself.
Goneril	The best and soundest of his time[2] hath been but rash . . .

[1] *obviously*
[2] *even at his most stable, when he was younger*

They are united in their determination: Lear must not be allowed to ruin their new-found power and status with further bouts of unpredictable behaviour, particularly as he will be living in their households from now on. The utmost strictness will be necessary.

Edmund states his case

I, ii

Edmund, illegitimate son of the Earl of Gloucester, is burning with resentment. He feels himself to be the victim of two meaningless social traditions: first, that illegitimate children are regarded as base and inferior; and second, that a father's property is inherited by the eldest son. On both counts, his brother Edgar has the advantage, and stands to inherit Gloucester's title and estate on his death.

Edmund has come up with a plan to trick his father into disinheriting Edgar. He has no scruples about the dishonesty that will be involved. The conventions of religion, morality and the law all seem to be against him, and he is determined to pursue his own interests ruthlessly:

Edmund   Thou, Nature, art my goddess; to thy law
My services are bound. Wherefore should I
Stand in the plague of custom,[1] and permit
The curiosity of nations[2] to deprive me . . .

[1] *respect traditions which I find hateful*
[2] *the pointless distinctions made by societies*

"Edmund, who refuses all moral rules and restraints, who does not recognise the very concept of morality, is the one who is made to underline the absolute moral responsibility for their own actions of everyone, himself included, in the play - and outside it."

C. W. R. D. Moseley, *Shakespeare's History Plays*, 1988

Far from feeling inferior to the legitimate Edgar, Edmund believes himself to be more spirited and forceful than his elder brother:

Edmund   Why brand they us
             With base? with baseness? bastardy? base, base?
             Who in the lusty stealth of nature take
             More composition and fierce quality[1]
             Than doth, within a dull, stale, tired bed,
             Go to th'creating a whole tribe of fops,[2]
             Got[3] 'tween asleep and wake? Well then,
             Legitimate Edgar, I must have your land . . .

> [1] *a more complete mixture of characteristics, and an*
>   *energetic nature*
> [2] *lifeless fools*
> [3] *conceived*

Edmund's plan to gain his father's inheritance involves a forged letter, which he has already prepared. The next step is to trick his father, Gloucester, into believing it to be genuine; and he is now approaching.

A shock for Gloucester

Gloucester is in a despondent mood. There seems to have been a sudden, inexplicable outbreak of madness in the court, what with Kent's banishment, the breaking off of relations with France, and Lear's voluntary handover of power.

As he comes across his son Edmund, Gloucester notices him hastily stuffing a letter into his pocket. He is curious to know what news it contains, and why he should want to hide it so urgently. Edmund at first denies the existence of the letter, thus arousing his father's curiosity even further.

Edmund then admits that he has a letter, from his brother Edgar; but he has only partly read it, he claims, and from what he has read is concerned that his father might find it offensive. By now Gloucester is determined to see the letter, and Edmund, with a show of unwillingness, hands it over. Gloucester reads:

> This policy and reverence of age makes the world bitter to the best of our times;[1] keeps our fortunes from us till our oldness cannot relish them . . . Come to me, that of this I may speak more. If our father would sleep till I wak'd him, you should enjoy half his revenue for ever, and live the beloved of your brother, EDGAR.

> [1] this tradition of respecting the old is a blight on our youth, which should be the best time of our lives

The message is unmistakeable. Edgar, impatient to inherit Gloucester's wealth, wants Edmund to collude with him in the murder of their father. If he agrees, Edgar will reward him with half the estate. Gloucester is horrified.

Edmund reluctantly admits that the handwriting appears to be his brother's, but he refuses to accept that Edgar really means what he has written. On the other hand, he remarks to Gloucester, he has often heard his brother voice the opinion that a son, when he comes of age, should take over the wealth of his ageing father and manage his affairs. Gloucester is convinced that the letter is genuine. Aghast at Edgar's treachery, he decides to have him seized immediately.

Edmund tries to calm his father down, and offers an alternative explanation: he believes that Edgar wrote him the letter to test his loyalty to their father. To prove this, he will arrange to meet Edgar and talk about the contents of the letter in a spot where Gloucester can overhear them. Edmund reassures his father that this will prove Edgar's innocence. Gloucester, desperate to know the truth, agrees to go along with the plan.

Gloucester foresees a bleak future

The whole episode has shaken Gloucester deeply. He is convinced, more than ever, that there is some malign power at work in the world. All these problems were foreshadowed by recent signs in the heavens, he believes:

Gloucester   These late eclipses in the sun and moon portend no good to us . . . Love cools, friendship falls off, brothers divide: in cities, mutinies; in countries, discord; in palaces, treason; and the bond crack'd 'twixt son and father. This villain of mine comes under the prediction;[1] there's son against father: the King falls from bias of nature;[2] there's father against child. We have seen the best of our time . . .[3]

[1] *Edgar's villainous behaviour is proof that the predictions are accurate*
[2] *the natural tendency to love one's child*
[3] *our best days are over*

Gloucester leaves, anxious and dejected. Edmund, pleased that his scheme is going according to plan, is greatly amused by the old man's faith in astrological predictions:

Edmund This is the excellent foppery[1] of the world, that, when we are sick in fortune, often the surfeits[2] of our own behaviour, we make guilty of our disasters the sun, the moon, and stars; as if we were villains on necessity, fools by heavenly compulsion . . .

[1] *foolishness*
[2] *results of excesses*

Edmund draws his brother into the plot

For the next stage of his plan, Edmund needs to ensure that his brother is in the right place this evening for the two of them to meet under Gloucester's observation. Edmund is in luck; Edgar is coming his way this very minute.

When Edgar arrives, Edmund puts on a thoughtful, worried air. He mentions the recent eclipses that Gloucester had been so concerned about; he fears they are portents of terrible events. Edgar is surprised to find that his brother is interested in astrology, and is amused that he appears to take it so seriously. Edmund immediately casts a cloud over his brother's good humour:

Edmund	When saw you my father last?
Edgar	The night gone by.
Edmund	Spake you with him?
Edgar	Ay, two hours together.
Edmund	Parted you in good terms? Found you no displeasure in him by word nor countenance?
Edgar	None at all.
Edmund	Bethink yourself[1] wherein you may have offended him . . .

[1] *try to work out, try to remember*

Somehow, Edmund warns him, Edgar has got himself into deep trouble with his father. The safest thing for him to do is to keep out of his father's way until his anger has died down. Edmund suggests his own lodgings as a hiding-place, and he hands him the key. Edgar, stunned at this sudden, dreadful turn of events, takes it.

If Edgar needs to leave his hiding-place, Edmund warns him, he must go armed and ready to defend himself. Edgar is almost speechless with horror. The situation is bad, warns Edmund, far worse than he has described; but he promises Edgar that he will do his best to help him.

As Edgar leaves, Edmund reflects triumphantly on his progress:

Edmund   A credulous father, and a brother noble,
Whose nature is so far from doing harms
That he suspects none; on whose foolish honesty
My practices ride easy! I see the business.[1]
Let me, if not by birth, have lands by wit:[2]
All with me's meet that I can fashion fit.[3]

[1] *what is necessary*
[2] *intelligence, cunning*
[3] *I don't mind what actions I need to take, as long
    as they serve my purposes*

---

*"Before the play begins, we are in roughly the upper world
of human nature; not a paradisal state, of course, but a world
where there is authority, social discipline, orders of distinction, and loyalty: the conditions regarded as the central ones
in the Tudor world. Then the dreaded image of the map appears, with a proposal to carve up the country . . . By the end
of the scene, we have the feeling of sliding into a different
world, and when Edmund steps forth we feel that he's the
first person to have recognised this world for what it is."*

Northrop Frye, *On Shakespeare*, 1986

Lear is proving unmanageable

I, iii

Lear is in residence at the palace of Albany and Goneril, who are now rulers of half the kingdom. With him is his retinue of a hundred knights and his Fool, the court jester who is allowed, by tradition, to say whatever he wants without fear of punishment.

Goneril is not happy with the current state of affairs. She finds Lear difficult and short-tempered, and his knights riotous and out of control. She instructs her steward Oswald to make a point of being surly and uncooperative in Lear's presence, and to show an unfriendly attitude to his attendants. She tells Oswald to instruct the other members of the household staff to behave in the same way.

Goneril's aim is to provoke Lear into complaining, and to bring the situation to a head so that she can confront him and demand an improvement in his behaviour. Lear may complain that his other daughter, Regan, will treat him more kindly, but Goneril knows that her sister's feelings will be exactly the same as her own. To be certain that the two of them take the same approach, Goneril intends to write to her sister immediately.

Kent rejoins Lear

I, iv

The Earl of Kent, banished for speaking out when Cordelia was disowned, has secretly followed Lear to Goneril's palace. He has disguised himself, and intends to assume a new accent and a new identity. He is determined to help Lear, whom he has loved and served loyally for many years.

As Lear returns from the hunt, accompanied by his knights and attendants, Kent approaches and attracts his attention. Lear questions the man. He is intrigued and amused by the stranger's blunt, simple answers. Since the stranger seems to be so determined to help him, Lear asks him what services he can offer. The man's reply pleases him:

Kent   I can keep honest counsel,[1] ride, run, mar a curious tale in telling it, and deliver a plain message bluntly; that which ordinary men are fit for, I am qualified in, and the best of me is diligence.

[1] *keep a secret, as long as it is honourable*

Lear agrees to take the man on.

> *"Kent's initial refusal to dissimulate in the matter of Cordelia's loyalty and love forces him, with bitter irony, into another kind of dissembling."*
>
> Anne Righter, *Shakespeare and the Idea of the Play*, 1962

Kent gains favour with the King

As instructed by Goneril, Oswald is behaving awkwardly. When Lear calls him, he wanders away without answering. Lear sends one of his knights after him, only to find that the steward refuses to come back and attend to him.

The knight suggests that Lear is not generally being treated with the love and respect to which he is accustomed. Lear too has noticed a change, and intends to talk to Goneril. For the present, though, he wants the company of his Fool, whom he has not seen for two days. He is distressed when the knight reminds him of the reason for the Fool's absence, and silences him abruptly:

Knight	Since my young Lady's[1] going into France, Sir, the Fool hath much pined away.
Lear	No more of that; I have noted it well.

[1] *Cordelia*

Oswald comes in again, and Lear calls him over. When the steward refers to him as Goneril's father, rather than the King, Lear becomes furious. He strikes Oswald: Kent then trips him, and the steward lands in an undignified heap. Kent chases him away. Lear is pleased with his new servant.

The Fool reminds Lear of his folly

At this point Lear's Fool arrives, chattering, joking and singing. Lear delights in the company of his Fool, and gives him free rein to pass comment on anything and anyone, even the King, as he pleases.

At present, the theme of all the Fool's comments is the same:

Lear's folly in giving all his power and wealth to his two dom-
ineering daughters, and nothing to Cordelia. The message is
sometimes hidden in a stream of cheerful, inane chatter, but the
Fool repeats it time and again.

Lear's tolerance of his Fool is in sharp contrast to Goneril's
distaste for his irreverent remarks:

Lear	And[1] you lie, sirrah, we'll have you whipp'd.
Fool	I marvel what kin thou and thy daughters are:
	they'll have me whipp'd for speaking true,
	thou'lt have me whipp'd for lying; and
	sometimes I am whipp'd for holding my peace.
	I had rather be any kind o'thing than a fool;
	and yet I would not be thee, Nuncle;[2] thou hast
	pared thy wit o'both sides, and left nothing
	i'th'middle . . .

[1] *if*
[2] *uncle (the Fool's nickname for Lear)*

Lear's Fool is not just a theatrical invention. The old
tradition of keeping fools was very much alive in Shakespeare's day. The fool - often physically or mentally
handicapped - was expected to be a continual source of
entertainment, and was allowed to make fun of anyone,
regardless of status. Fools were not only kept for amusement: they were also believed to ward off evil spirits
and bring good luck.

Fools were employed in establishments of all sorts, rang-
ing from the court of Elizabeth I to private households,
taverns and brothels. The tradition did not die out until
well into the 18th century.

A confrontation

Goneril enters. It is clear from her expression that she is far from happy:

Lear   How now, daughter! what makes that frontlet[1] on? You are too much of late i'th'frown.

> [1] *ornamental headband: referring, ironically, to Goneril's continual frown*

The Fool continues to chatter, but Goneril silences him with a glare. She turns to her father and delivers an angry but carefully-worded statement. His companions are noisy, argumentative and insolent: she strongly suspects that Lear, far from keeping them under control, is tolerating and even encouraging their riotous behaviour. If this proves to be the case, she will feel perfectly justified in dealing with him harshly, and will not hesitate to do so.

Lear is dumbfounded to hear his own daughter address him in this way. For a moment he is overcome by a sense of unreality: this cannot be his daughter; perhaps he himself is no longer King Lear.

Goneril persists. She is not asking for anything unreasonable, she claims, and is interested in his peace of mind as well as her own. The first priority is to cut down the number of his companions:

Goneril   ... As you are old and reverend, should be
            wise.
        Here do you keep a hundred knights and
            squires;
        Men so disorder'd, so debosh'd,[1] and bold,
        That this our court, infected with their
            manners,
        Shows like a riotous inn ...
                            ... be then desir'd
        By her, that else will take the thing she begs,
        A little to disquantity your train;
        And the remainders, that shall still depend,[2]
        To be such men as may besort[3] your age,
        Which know themselves and you.

[1] *debauched*
[2] *remain as your followers*
[3] *suit*

In short, Lear must dismiss half his followers. Lear's astonishment now turns to fury. He calls out for his horses to be saddled and his company to be assembled: they are to leave immediately for Regan's palace, where he expects to be treated with proper hospitality. His knights are men of honour and distinction, he insists: in trying to curb his followers, Goneril is guilty of meanness and ingratitude.

It is more than Lear can bear. Beside himself with anger, he cries out for Nature to make Goneril suffer as he is suffering:

Lear   If she must teem,[1]
            Create her child of spleen, that it may live
            And be a thwart disnatur'd[2] torment to her!
            Let it stamp wrinkles in her brow of youth,
            With cadent tears fret channels in her cheeks,
            Turn all her mother's pains and benefits
            To laughter and contempt, that she may feel
            How sharper than a serpent's tooth it is
            To have a thankless child!

> [1] *bear children*
> [2] *perverse and unnatural*

The Duke of Albany, who has just entered, tries to pacify Lear and establish what is going on. Lear, frantic to the point of tears, ignores him and storms out, followed by his faithful Fool.

Albany did not witness the start of Lear's emotional outburst, but he suspects that Goneril may have been too drastic. Mild and tolerant by nature, he would prefer not to have taken the behaviour of Lear and his knights as such a threat. His wife disagrees:

Albany   . . . you may fear too far.
Goneril   Safer than trust too far.

Goneril sends her steward Oswald to Regan, to deliver a letter in which she describes her fears about their father, and the reduction in his train that she proposes. Albany is anxious; his wife's severity in dealing with the situation, he fears, may only make it worse.

Lear sets off to join Regan

I, v

Outside Goneril's palace, Lear is preparing to leave. His destination is the household of Regan and the Duke of Cornwall, where he intends to take up residence with his followers. He sends Kent ahead, to deliver a letter to Regan as quickly as possible.

In the Fool's enigmatic utterances is the suggestion that their welcome there may not be any warmer than at Goneril's home, but Lear ignores the hint. He is only half listening to his Fool; he is preoccupied with Goneril's ingratitude and his own treatment of Cordelia. His mind is in turmoil, and he is starting to fear for his sanity:

Lear   O! let me not be mad, not mad, sweet heaven;
                Keep me in temper; I would not be mad!

Once the horses are ready, and his companions assembled, Lear sets out on his hopeful journey. The Fool, unheeded, warns that it will all end in tears.

Edmund plans to drive his brother into hiding

II, i

At the Earl of Gloucester's castle, Edmund is continuing with his plot against his older brother Edgar. It is now late in the evening, and Edgar has been hiding in Edmund's room since hearing of his father's terrible wrath earlier in the day.

Edmund realises that he must be extremely careful. It is essential that Edgar and Gloucester do not meet; if they do, the truth about the forged letter will emerge. And the scenario he promised his father - that he and Edgar would talk about the letter while Gloucester eavesdropped - is clearly impossible.

What Edmund intends to do instead is to persuade Edgar to flee. Once Edgar has had time to escape from the castle into the surrounding country, Edmund can raise the alarm and tell his father that the letter was, as he had feared, genuine. His hope is that Edgar will be forced to stay in hiding indefinitely. In any case, Gloucester is certain to place a price on his disloyal son's head: there is a good chance that Edgar will be summarily executed by anyone who finds him.

Edmund is now outside the room where his brother is hiding, and is about to urge him to flee. However, at this point one of Gloucester's courtiers approaches and passes on some news: Regan and her husband, the Duke of Cornwall, are coming to the castle this very night. There is a rumour, he adds, that war between Cornwall and Albany, the two rulers of the divided kingdom, is imminent.

Edgar decides to use this information to his advantage. He will have to think quickly.

Edgar makes his escape

Edmund calls his brother down from his hiding-place. The situation is desperate, he tells him: someone has informed their father of Edgar's whereabouts, and he will be seized unless he escapes immediately.

Before Edgar has a chance to speak, Edmund reveals that it is not only Gloucester who holds a grudge against him; the Duke of Cornwall himself is on his way to the castle, hurrying through the dark, this very minute. He implores Edgar to try to remember what he has said about Cornwall that may have caused offence. The innocent Edgar, more terrified and confused than ever, denies having spoken about the Duke. There is no time to spare, urges Edmund: he must run away immediately.

Edmund draws his sword and tells his brother to do the same: it is essential that they appear to be fighting; there is no time to explain why. Bewildered, Edgar obeys, and the two of them cross swords. As they fight, Edmund orders him to stand where he can be seen by Gloucester, who is now approaching. Finally he tells him to flee, and Edgar runs off into the night.

Gloucester passes judgement on his son

Before Gloucester arrives, Edmund wounds his own arm with his sword, drawing blood, to demonstrate the violent struggle that has just taken place. The next minute his father arrives on the scene. Without delay he asks Edmund where his brother has fled to. To ensure that Edgar has time to escape from the castle, Edmund does not answer immediately.

Instead, he feigns a state of shock, and starts to describe what has just happened, playing on his father's superstitious beliefs:

Gloucester	Now, Edmund, where's the villain?
Edmund	Here stood he in the dark, his sharp sword out,
	Mumbling of wicked charms, conjuring[1] the moon
	To stand auspicious mistress.[2]
Gloucester	But where is he?
Edmund	Look, Sir, I bleed.

[1] *appealing to, praying to*
[2] *to give her blessing to his plans*

Edmund finally shows the direction in which Edgar has fled, and Gloucester sends his attendants off at once in pursuit. Edmund then reveals to his father the full story of what has just happened. Edgar has just tried to persuade him to collaborate in Gloucester's murder: when he refused, Edgar attacked him without warning, gashing his arm. When Edmund drew his sword in defence, and cried out for help, Edgar fled.

Gloucester's worst fears are confirmed. He announces, gravely, that Edgar will be put to death as soon as he is found. In his search for his son, he will enlist the help of his ruler, the Duke of Cornwall, who is due to arrive shortly.

> *"Thus the tragic chain of events is set in motion: the two fathers have renounced the children who love them, and elected to trust the children who will betray them. Each has repudiated the natural bond and, horribly erring, cited 'nature' herself as the authority for his action."*
>
> John Wain, *The Living World of Shakespeare*, 1964

Edmund is rewarded

Edmund now adds another detail to his description. During his conversation with his brother, he tells Gloucester, he had threatened to make Edgar's plan public once it was clear that he could not be dissuaded. He remembers Edgar's reply word for word:

Edmund   . . . I threaten'd to discover him: he replied,
            'Thou unpossessing bastard! dost thou think,
            If I would stand against thee, would the reposal
            Of any trust, virtue, or worth in thee
            Make thy words faith'd?[1] No: what I should
                deny, -
            As this I would; ay, though thou didst produce
            My very character[2] - I'ld turn it all
            To thy suggestion, plot and damned
                practice . . .'[3]

            [1]   believed
            [2]   something written in my own handwriting
            [3]   I'd claim that any evidence you found against me
                  was the result of your own scheming and
                  fabrication

Gloucester, utterly convinced of the treachery and deviousness of his elder son, now speaks the words that Edmund has been waiting to hear:

Gloucester   . . . of my land,
            Loyal and natural boy, I'll work the means[1]
            To make thee capable.[2]

            [1]   I'll do what is necessary
            [2]   able to inherit

Edmund's plan has worked perfectly. He stands to inherit his father's land: Edgar is likely to be executed if he ever appears in public again: and if Edgar should be captured and brought before Gloucester, his pleas of innocence will not be believed.

Gloucester receives important visitors

Cornwall and Regan arrive at Gloucester's castle. They are shocked to hear the news that Gloucester's own son - who is also Lear's godson - has been plotting to murder him.

Somehow, Regan is under the illusion that the gentle Edgar had been keeping company with Lear's disorderly crowd of knights. That would account for his behaviour, she believes; she has just heard from her sister Goneril about their atrocious behaviour. Edmund volunteers the information that Edgar had indeed been spending time with Lear's followers.

Cornwall reassures Gloucester that everything possible will be done to track down his treacherous son. He then turns to Edmund, whose loyalty in defending his father has not gone unnoticed:

Cornwall   For you, Edmund,
            Whose virtue and obedience doth this instant
            So much commend itself, you shall be ours:
            Natures of such deep trust we shall much need;
            You we first seize on.

Edmund is to become the Duke's right-hand man. The Duke is already ruler of half of Britain: if the rumour that Edmund heard earlier is true, there is a chance that he may take over the entire kingdom.

Regan then explains why they have come to Gloucester's castle so late at night, and at such short notice. She has received urgent letters from both Lear and Goneril about their recent quarrels: she requires Gloucester's advice in preparing her replies. Gloucester is delighted to be of service to the Duke and his wife.

Although she does not mention it to Gloucester, Regan is in fact determined to be away from her home when Lear and his companions arrive, to emphasise that he cannot expect better treatment from her than from Goneril.

Kent's anger gets the better of him

II, ii

Kent, the messenger who delivered Lear's letter to Regan, and Oswald, who delivered Goneril's, have both been instructed to follow Regan through the night. The two men now meet outside Gloucester's castle.

Although Oswald does not recognise Kent, Kent recognises him: he is Goneril's steward, who recently incurred Lear's wrath, for which Kent tripped him up and hurled abuse at him. Kent feels an instinctive hostility towards the man which he is unable to suppress, and he launches a torrent of insults at the bewildered steward. As his anger grows, he challenges Oswald to a sword fight. What outrages Kent most is that the man is unashamedly acting against Lear's interests:

Kent   Draw, you rascal; you come with letters against
                the King, and take Vanity the puppet's[1] part
                against the royalty of her father. Draw, you
                rogue, or I'll so carbonado[2] your shanks . . .

> [1] *Goneril, whom he compares to a stock character in a puppet-show*
> [2] *cut into pieces, ready for stewing*

Unable to get his opponent to draw his sword, Kent beats him soundly, and Oswald cries out for help. Hearing the commotion, Edmund comes out from the castle with his sword drawn. Assuming him to be taking Oswald's side, Kent turns on him and challenges him to fight. Cornwall, Regan and Gloucester now all come out into the night.

Cornwall orders an end to the disturbance, and tries to establish the cause of the quarrel between the two messengers. He does not recognise the Earl of Kent, who is still disguised both

in appearance and accent. Oswald's claim that he has spared his
opponent's life in view of his great age rouses Kent's fury again:

Kent	My Lord, if you will give me leave, I will tread this unbolted[1] villain into mortar, and daub the wall of a jakes[2] with him . . .
Cornwall	Peace, sirrah! You beastly knave, know you no reverence?
Kent	Yes, sir; but anger hath a privilege.

[1] *one who deserves to be locked up: of mortar, coarse and of poor quality*
[2] *toilet, privy*

Cornwall and Gloucester continue to try to find out what
the argument is about. Kent, who prides himself on being blunt
and straightforward, can only insist repeatedly on his loathing
for Oswald, whom he sees as smooth, sycophantic and dishon-
est.

> *"In Shakespeare's day, the newly prosperous gentry and the commercially active bourgeoisie were rising in prosperity and power, largely at the expense of the old aristocracy. This conflict is plainly the cause of the extraordinary venom displayed by Kent towards Oswald. Oswald is a caricature of a 17th-century social climber . . ."*
>
> Charles Boyce, *Shakespeare A to Z*, 1990

Kent is punished

Cornwall, unimpressed by Kent's bluntness, becomes impatient. Finally, since Kent cannot give a good reason for assaulting Goneril's steward, Cornwall orders him to be put in the stocks outside the castle gate.

Kent protests. If this is a way of teaching him a lesson, he says, it is pointless; he is too old to learn. Besides, he is a servant of the King. Cornwall is unrepentant. He commands that Kent is to stay in the stocks for the remainder of the night and all the following morning. Regan breaks in. This is not long enough, she insists: he must stay there for the whole day tomorrow, and the whole of tomorrow night too.

Gloucester suggests, respectfully, that the punishment is rather too harsh and degrading for the King's messenger; Lear may be offended. Regan retorts that Goneril will no doubt be equally offended when she learns that her steward Oswald has been assaulted for no good reason. Kent is put in the stocks.

When Cornwall and Regan go back into the castle, the Earl stays behind for a private word with the messenger. He disapproves of Cornwall's action, he says, and will try to have him released. Kent reassures Gloucester that he can cope with the punishment.

On his own, Kent sits and waits for the dawn. He reveals that he earlier received a letter from Cordelia; she has learnt of the fact that he has rejoined the King in disguise. He has not yet read the contents, but he knows that she hopes somehow to restore Lear to happiness. When the sun rises, he will read the letter: for the time being, he sleeps.

Edgar takes on a new identity

II, iii

Edgar has escaped capture by hiding in a tree. Nowhere is safe: wherever he goes, he overhears voices calling for his arrest. If he is to remain free he must disguise himself. He has no money, no friends and nowhere to live, and the disguise he chooses is the lowliest he can imagine:

Edgar   . . . I will preserve myself; and am bethought
To take the basest and most poorest shape
That ever penury,[1] in contempt of man,
Brought near to beast; my face I'll grime with
      filth,
Blanket my loins, elf[2] all my hairs in knots,
And with presented nakedness outface[3]
The winds and persecutions of the sky.

[1] *poverty, destitution*
[2] *tangle: twist into elf-locks (knots in hair believed to be caused by elves)*
[3] *defy*

He will no longer be Edgar, son of the Earl of Gloucester, but Poor Tom, mad, homeless, filthy and rejected.

"The necessity for the adoption of disguise, or false identity, in order to remain oneself is one of the most painful paradoxes of King Lear.*"*

Anne Righter, *Shakespeare and the Idea of the Play*, 1962

Lear keeps his temper at bay

II, iv

Arriving at Regan's palace, with his train of knights, Lear is disconcerted to find that Regan and the Duke had unexpectedly left only hours before. He follows them to Gloucester's castle, and receives a further shock when he finds his messenger in the stocks outside the castle gate. It is now evening; Kent has been in the stocks all day.

When Kent tells Lear that it was his own daughter and son-in-law who put him in the stocks, Lear at first refuses to believe him. Kent explains the circumstances: irritated that Goneril's messenger was treated with greater courtesy than himself, and driven by sheer animosity, he attacked the man, and ended up in the stocks. Lear senses that he is about to be overcome yet again with a fit of uncontrollable fury. He forces himself to remain calm, and goes in search of his daughter Regan.

Kent notices that Lear's retinue of knights seems to be smaller than before. The Fool will not give him a straight answer, but hints that some of his followers, believing that the King's fortunes are on the way down, have deserted him.

Regan and Cornwall do not wish to speak to Lear immediately. They instruct Gloucester to put him off for a while, by telling him that they are exhausted after their long journey.

Lear is staggered: he has given a command, and expects to be obeyed, not fobbed off with excuses. Anger starts to well up inside him again, and again he tries to calm himself down; perhaps their excuse is genuine. But the sight of Kent in the stocks catches his eye again, and he is convinced that Regan and Cornwall are deliberately slighting him. He sends Gloucester back to demand their presence. The Fool comments wryly on Lear's continual attempts to control his temper:

Lear	O me! my heart, my rising heart! but, down!
Fool	Cry to it, Nuncle, as the cockney did to the
	eels when she put 'em i'th'paste alive; she
	knapp'd 'em o'th'coxcombs[1] with a stick, and
	cried 'Down, wantons,[2] down!'

[1] *rapped them on the head*
[2] *unruly creatures*

Lear sees an end to his troubles

Cornwall and Regan now agree to see Lear. They come out to greet him, and order Kent to be set free from the stocks.

Overflowing with emotion, Lear tells Regan how relieved he is to see her, and how he has been mistreated by her sister Goneril. Regan's response is cool and measured:

Regan	If, Sir, perchance
	She have restrain'd the riots of your followers,
	'Tis on such ground, and to such wholesome
	end,
	As clears her from all blame.
Lear	My curses on her!
Regan	O, Sir! you are old;
	Nature in you stands on the very verge
	Of her confine:[1] you should be rul'd and led
	By some discretion that discerns your state
	Better than you yourself. Therefore I pray you
	That to our sister you do make return . . .

[1] *limit; the span of time assigned to life*

This is the opposite of what Lear had hoped to hear from his daughter. Returning to Goneril is unthinkable. Remembering her intolerance and ingratitude, he becomes agitated again, calling on all the powers of nature to render Goneril sick, ugly and old:

Lear   Strike her young bones,
                    You taking[1] airs, with lameness!
                                        . . . Infect her beauty,
                    You fen-suck'd[2] fogs, drawn by the pow'rful
                        sun,
                    To fall and blister her!

> [1] *infecting, blighting*
> [2] *rising up from marshes*

Regan will treat him differently, he insists; she is gentle, tolerant and tender-hearted. Out of the love she naturally feels for her father, and her gratitude for her inheritance, she will welcome him and his followers, and all will be well. He refuses to believe otherwise. Regan's words have still not sunk in.

Regan and Goneril unite

Lear is determined to know who put his messenger in the stocks. He is sure that it cannot have been Regan or the Duke of Cornwall, who would not have shown him such disrespect. But before he can receive an answer, another visitor arrives at Gloucester's castle: it is Goneril, who has arranged to meet Regan here so that they can confront their father together.

Seeing Goneril appear before him again, bold and shameless, Lear is filled with indignation. He is even more horrified when Regan takes her sister's hand in friendship: and he reels from yet another blow when her husband Cornwall states that it was he who put Lear's servant in the stocks.

Regan now addresses Lear calmly and firmly. He must return to Goneril's palace and, as she asked, dismiss half his followers. He can then come, as arranged, to live with Regan the following month. Lear refuses absolutely. It is inconceivable that he should go back to Goneril, whom he never wishes to see again. Although she is a constant source of anguish to him, he tells Goneril, he does not care whether she changes her ways or not: he can live in contentment, with his companions, at Regan's palace.

Regan makes it plain that this is not so. She sees Goneril's point of view, she explains: he does not need his hundred knights when both sisters have plenty of attendants to look after him. Like Goneril, she will demand a reduction in his following. In fact, Goneril's limit of fifty is too high: if Lear intends to stay with her, Regan states, he may only bring twenty-five of his knights.

Lear is now reduced to a pitiful, childish state, haggling pathetically over the number of companions he is allowed: his plight is made all the more poignant by the fact that many of his followers have in fact already deserted him. He will return to Goneril, he declares petulantly. The sisters close in together:

Lear	[*To Goneril.*] I'll go with thee:
	Thy fifty yet doth double five-and-twenty,
	And thou art twice her love.
Goneril	Hear me, my Lord.
	What need you five-and-twenty, ten, or five,
	To follow in a house where twice so many
	Have a command to tend you?
Regan	What need one?

Lear will be accepted in their households as an old, solitary man, but not as a King with his entourage of knights.

A storm approaches

Distressed at being dragged into a squalid argument about numbers, Lear cries out in exasperation:

Lear   O! reason not the need;[1] our basest beggars
             Are in the poorest thing superfluous:[2]
             Allow not nature more than nature needs,[3]
             Man's life is cheap as beast's.

             [1] *don't analyse things from the point of view of*
                  whether they are necessary or not
             [2] *have more than is necessary for bare existence*
             [3] *if you do not allow people to enjoy more than the*
                  basic necessities

He tells his daughters that they are hypocritical in trying to restrict him purely to what he needs; they take far more trouble over their own clothes, for example, than is dictated by mere necessity.

On the verge of tears, he calls on the gods to give him patience. He wants to rid himself of the bitter, impotent rage that continually overwhelms him: he wants his anger to be powerful, majestic and feared. But his attempt to threaten his daughters with vengeance, as he sets off with his Fool, falls into pathos:

Lear   . . . you unnatural hags,
I will have such revenges on you both
That all the world shall - I will do such things,
What they are, yet I know not, but they shall
        be
The terrors of the earth. You think I'll weep;
No, I'll not weep:
I have full cause of weeping, but this heart
Shall break into a hundred thousand flaws[1]
Or ere[2] I'll weep. O Fool! I shall go mad.

[1] *fragments*
[2] *before*

Goneril and Regan, satisfied that they are in the right, do not attempt to stop Lear as he rushes out. Gloucester is concerned. There is no shelter for miles around, the night is coming on, and a storm is approaching; thunder can already be heard rumbling in the distance.

Cornwall suggests that Lear should be allowed to go where he wants. Goneril tells Gloucester, pointedly, not to try to stop him. Regan backs them both up: Lear must learn from his own mistakes, she explains. Finally, Gloucester's master Cornwall advises him to shut all his doors securely; it will be a wild night. Gloucester reluctantly obeys. The doors are closed against the oncoming storm. Lear is locked out.

> "*For many of us today,* King Lear *seems the uttermost reach of Shakespeare's achievement. As compared with* Hamlet, *the nineteenth century's favourite,* King Lear *speaks of a world more problematical* . . . King Lear's *world, like our century, is larger, looser, cruder, crueller.*"
>
> Maynard Mack, *Everybody's Shakespeare*, 1993

France prepares to invade

III, i

On an open heath, in the raging storm, Kent is searching for Lear, who has rushed out into the turbulent night with only his Fool for company. He comes across a man whom he recognises as a trusted member of the old King's court, when Lear had been in power. Kent, his appearance and accent both disguised, remains unrecognised.

The gentleman does not know where Lear is now, but has seen him recently, battling in vain against the storm:

Kent	Where's the King?
Gentleman	Contending with the fretful elements;
	Bids the wind blow the earth into the sea,
	Or swell the curled waters 'bove the main,[1]
	That things might change or cease; tears his white hair,
	Which the impetuous blasts, with eyeless rage,
	Catch in their fury, and make nothing of;[2]
	Strives in his little world of man to out-storm
	The to-and-fro conflicting wind and rain.

[1] *land*
[2] *scatter into oblivion*

Kent discloses some important, confidential information to the gentleman. Cordelia's husband, the King of France, has spies amongst the household servants of both rulers of Britain, the Dukes of Albany and Cornwall. They have informed France of quarrels between the two men which have not yet come out into the open, but which are likely to lead to a serious rift between the two halves of the kingdom. In the meantime, France has secretly dispatched troops to a number of British ports and is preparing for a full-scale invasion, with the objective of uniting the kingdom and restoring Lear to power. One contingent of troops is in Dover: Cordelia is with them.

Kent instructs the gentleman to make his way to Dover. He must make Lear's recent treatment known to the King's supporters, and encourage them to press on with the invasion. He gives the gentleman his ring; Cordelia will recognise it, he assures him, and will know that the message is genuine. The first priority, however, is to find Lear and bring him to safety. Both men set off into the night in search of the King.

> "What must have struck some of Shakespeare's contemporaries . . . was that here a structure they had long associated with pastoral romance, the most popular of their literary and dramatic genres, had been turned topsy-turvy and charged with undreamed-of power . . . the scenes on the heath are the greatest anti-pastoral ever penned."
>
> Maynard Mack, *Everybody's Shakespeare*, 1993

Lear confronts the storm

III, ii

In the midst of the wild, blustery storm, Lear is howling in anguish. He calls on the raging elements to fall upon him, and to devastate the world, turning its orderliness to chaos, destruction and sterility:

Lear   Blow, winds, and crack your cheeks! rage! blow!
You cataracts and hurricanoes,[1] spout
Till you have drench'd our steeples, drown'd the cocks![2]
You sulph'rous and thought-executing fires,[3]
Vaunt-couriers[4] of oak-cleaving thunderbolts,
Singe my white head! And thou, all-shaking thunder,
Strike flat the thick rotundity o'th'world!

[1] *waterspouts, sucked out of the sea by whirlwinds*
[2] *weathercocks*
[3] *lightning-flashes, moving as fast as thought*
[4] *heralds, forerunners*

The Fool tries to persuade Lear to go back to the shelter of Gloucester's castle, even if it means giving in to Goneril and Regan. Lear ignores him, and continues to call on the storm to do its worst: its impersonal, heedless violence is preferable to the malice of his daughters:

Lear   Rumble thy bellyful![1] Spit, fire! spout, rain!
        Nor rain, wind, thunder, fire, are my daughters:
        I tax[2] you not, you elements, with unkindness;
        I never gave you kingdom, call'd you children,
        You owe me no subscription:[3] then let fall
        Your horrible pleasure; here I stand, your slave,
        A poor, infirm, weak, and despis'd old man.

[1] *as much as you want*
[2] *charge, accuse*
[3] *obedience, loyalty*

Eventually, drained and weary, Lear falls into an uneasy silence. He will be patient, he tells himself: but for all his wild roaring, and the storm's ferocious battering, he has still not rid himself of his burning sense of injustice and anger.

Lear accuses mankind

Kent, wandering across the dark, unsheltered heath, finally discovers Lear and his Fool. He tells Lear that he must get out of the storm: this is the roughest, most violent night in living memory, and he will not be able to survive much longer out in the open.

Lear is oblivious. His uncontrollable anger bursts out again, but now it is the whole mass of corrupt humanity, not just his daughters, who are the target of his indignation. He cries out for the storm to continue, shattering all the world's hypocrisy and laying bare the countless hidden crimes that go undetected:

Lear   Let the great Gods,
That keep this dreadful pudder[1] o'er our heads,
Find out their enemies now. Tremble, thou
    wretch,
That hast within thee undivulged crimes,
Unwhipp'd of[2] Justice; hide thee, thou bloody
    hand,
Thou perjur'd, and thou simular[3] of virtue
That art incestuous . . .
                I am a man
More sinn'd against than sinning.

[1] *turmoil, commotion*
[2] *by*
[3] *counterfeiter, one who plays a part*

Kent persists. He has found a hovel on the heath that will provide shelter from the worst of the storm: Lear must take refuge there at once. Lear, calming down, becomes aware of the reality of his situation. He senses that his mental stability is at risk in all this emotional and physical upheaval.

Noticing his Fool shivering with cold, Lear takes pity on him: it occurs to him that he is cold himself. He follows Kent to the hovel.

> *"In Act III of* King Lear *we witness the emergence and gradual ascendance of Lear's soul . . . He gradually leaves off playing the ruler of the elements and begins to treat the people around him with humble courtesy, feeling for the first time the continuity of humanity."*
>
> Germaine Greer, *Shakespeare*, 1986

> "*The play offers disconcerting suggestions of comedy that complicate our response and thus increase its emotional power. In* King Lear *Shakespeare employed a number of elements traditionally associated with comedy: a double plot; the use of a jester to comment on the action; the use of disguise; the progression of the action from royal court to country and back to court; and the counterpoint of youth and age.*"
>
> Charles Boyce, *Shakespeare A to Z*, 1990

Gloucester stands by the King

III, iii

Inside the castle, Gloucester is talking confidentially to his son Edmund. He is deeply unhappy about the way Lear has been treated. He has been expressly forbidden to help Lear in any way, and is not even allowed to offer his own home as shelter. Edmund is shocked; as he points out, it is a most unnatural way for Lear's own daughters to behave.

Gloucester continues. There has been an extremely serious development in the kingdom, he tells his son; on no account must he mention it to anyone else. The first stages of an invasion are under way. The invading forces, taking advantage of conflicts between the two Dukes, have already set foot in Britain; their intention is to unite the kingdom once more under the rule of King Lear.

He and his son will naturally support the old King, says Gloucester, but they must keep their support an absolute secret; the Duke himself is still present in the castle. Gloucester has received a letter telling him of the progress of the invasion, which he has locked away securely in his room.

Gloucester intends to go out into the storm to find Lear and provide him with food and shelter. The ultimate aim is to get the King to Dover, the principal base of the invading army, where his loyal daughter Cordelia is present. To avoid arousing suspicion, it is vital that Gloucester's absence, while he goes out to search for Lear, is not noticed. He tells Edmund to engage the Duke in conversation and distract his attention; if he asks after Gloucester, Edmund must explain that he is ill and in bed.

When Gloucester has left, Edmund's true feelings become apparent. He is delighted at this easy opportunity for advancement, and intends to tell the Duke at once of the letter hidden in his father's room. Cornwall's displeasure towards Gloucester is likely to be matched by his gratitude to Edmund:

Edmund   ... This seems a fair deserving,[1] and must draw me
That which my father loses; no less than all:
The younger rises when the old doth fall.

[1] *an act that will deserve to be rewarded*

Lear succumbs to madness

III, iv

Outside, the storm continues. Lear and his Fool, guided by Kent, have reached the derelict hovel in which they can take shelter. Kent urges Lear to enter. Lear hesitates. He hardly notices the cold, the biting wind, the rain and thunder; if anything, the storm comforts him, matching the tempestuous state of his own emotions and helping to block out consideration of his daughters' ingratitude.

Realising the suffering that Kent and the Fool are going through as they wait outside the hovel, he takes pity on them and tells them to go in ahead of him. As his Fool takes cover, Lear is overcome with a wave of sympathy for the poor and the homeless everywhere, as he imagines them trying to cope with this storm. He should have helped them more, he realises, when he was in power:

Lear   Poor naked wretches, wheresoe'er you are,
That bide[1] the pelting of this pitiless storm,
How shall your houseless heads and unfed sides,
Your loop'd and window'd[2] raggedness, defend
     you
From seasons such as these? O! I have ta'en
Too little care of this. Take physic, Pomp;[3]
Expose thyself to feel what wretches feel,
That thou mayst shake the superflux[4] to them,
And show the heavens more just.

[1] *endure*
[2] *full of rips and holes*
[3] *take this treatment, those of you in authority*
[4] *excess wealth*

Expose thyself to feel what wretches feel . . .

The earliest known performance of *King Lear* was at the court of King James I in 1606, about a year after the Gunpowder Plot. It is possible that Shakespeare was writing the play at the time of the discovery of the plot and the arrest of Guy Fawkes.

"Enhanced by the richest dramatic poetry Shakespeare ever produced, King Lear *nevertheless predicates the transition from the old feudal role of kingship to a new accommodation of the King's subjects . . . Reduced to nothing but a retrospect on kingship, Lear offers food for thought to a reigning monarch whose narrow escape from being blown up in the House of Commons was the sensation of 1605."*

Peter Thomson, *Shakespeare's Professional Career*, 1992

The Fool, having just gone into the hovel, suddenly runs out screaming. There's a ghost inside, he warns; and bizarre cries can be heard from under the straw in the squalid hut. Kent orders the spirit to come outside. A filthy, ragged, half-naked creature, uttering wild cries, emerges into the storm.

It is Edgar, in his disguise as Poor Tom, the mad beggar. Hiding from his father's vengeance, in constant fear of being found and recognised, he too has ended up on the wild, stormy heath. To reinforce his disguise, he keeps up a constant stream of lunatic ranting.

Lear, his own sanity by now giving way, takes to the grotesque stranger at once. It is clear to him that Poor Tom, like himself, has lost everything to his daughters: he refuses to accept any other explanation. Impressed by his covering of a single, shabby blanket, Lear decides that Poor Tom has achieved an ideal state of purity and simplicity. He too, he decides, must strip himself of the unnecessary trappings of civilisation:

Lear   Consider him well. Thou ow'st the worm no silk, the beast no hide, the sheep no wool, the cat no perfume. Ha! here's three on's are sophisticated;[1] thou art the thing itself; unaccommodated[2] man is no more but such a poor, bare, forked[3] animal as thou art. Off, off, you lendings! Come; unbutton here.

[1] *the three of us (Lear, Kent and the Fool) are artificial and unnatural*
[2] *without the veneer of civilisation*
[3] *two-legged*

Still at the mercy of the storm, Lear starts to tear his clothes off with demented energy.

Gloucester brings Lear out of the storm

The Earl of Gloucester now arrives. He is dismayed to find the King in the company of a foul, mad, ranting beggar. He tells Lear that, despite his daughters' injunction, he has prepared a room for him, with a fire and food for his comfort.

Told that Lear's sanity is deteriorating, Gloucester reflects, gloomily, that he is not surprised. The Earl of Kent, he remembers, predicted the awful consequences that would come about on the fateful occasion when Lear gave all to Goneril and Regan and nothing to Cordelia. He himself, he confides, has been driven to the verge of madness by his own son, who recently tried to take his life. He does not realise that the two men of whom he speaks, Kent and Edgar, are both with him now, in disguise.

Gloucester urges Lear to come with him, and tells Poor Tom the beggar to go back into the hovel. But Lear will not be parted from his new-found friend, whose bizarre outbursts he regards as the height of wisdom. Gloucester agrees to let the pitiful vagrant come with them, and they make their way across the dark, stormy heath to warmth and shelter.

Gloucester's fate is sealed

III, v

Edmund has informed the Duke of Cornwall of the letter hidden in his father's room. The Duke has found it: the contents reveal that an invasion from France is secretly under way, and make it clear that Gloucester is taking the side of France in the bid to restore the old King and remove the present rulers.

Cornwall's first thought is revenge. The Earl of Gloucester must be captured and punished. Edmund maintains an air of pain and distress; he is torn, he tells the Duke, between his love for his father and his desire to do his duty. Cornwall reassures him that he has done the right thing.

Edmund's plan has come to fruition, even more quickly than he had hoped:

Edmund   If the matter of this paper[1] be certain, you have
            mighty business in hand.
Cornwall   True or false, it hath made thee Earl of
            Gloucester.

> [1]   the news of the invasion

Cornwall orders Edmund to search for his treacherous father. Edmund, with a display of reluctance, obeys. Again Cornwall reassures him; from now on, the Duke himself will be like a father to him.

Lear stages a trial

III, vi

Gloucester leads the mad King and his little group of followers to an outbuilding near the castle. Once they are safely inside, he returns immediately to the castle.

Lear, in his deluded state, decides to hold a trial of Goneril
and Regan. Poor Tom, still gibbering wildly, is to be judge: the
Fool is to sit next to him on the bench. Lear ignores Kent's plea
for him to rest, and calls for Goneril to be brought before the
court. He sees Goneril appear before him, with Regan following: then, in his hallucination, he sees Goneril escape, and cries
out in rage.

Kent is dismayed at his old master's disturbed state of mind,
and Edgar is so upset that he finds it difficult to keep up his
pretence:

Fool	Come hither, mistress. Is your name Goneril?
Lear	She cannot deny it.
Fool	Cry you mercy, I took[1] you for a joint-stool.
Lear	And here's another, whose warp'd looks proclaim
	What store[2] her heart is made on. Stop her there!
	Arms, arms, sword, fire! Corruption in the place!
	False justicer, why hast thou let her 'scape?
Edgar	Bless thy five wits!

Kent　　　　　O pity! Sir, where is the patience now
　　　　　　　That you so oft have boasted to retain?
Edgar　　　　[*aside*] My tears begin to take his part so much,
　　　　　　　They mar my counterfeiting.

　　　¹　*mistook*
　　　²　*stuff, material*

Since Goneril has escaped, Lear turns to Regan: but instead of trying her, he proposes the dissection of her body. His attention then wanders to Poor Tom in his blanket:

Lear　　　　　. . . let them anatomize Regan, see what breeds¹
　　　　　　　about her heart. Is there any cause in nature
　　　　　　　that make these hard hearts? [*To Edgar.*] You,
　　　　　　　sir, I entertain for one of my hundred;² only I
　　　　　　　do not like the fashion of your garments: you
　　　　　　　will say they are Persian;³ but let them be
　　　　　　　chang'd.

　　　¹　*hatches, grows*
　　　²　*retinue of a hundred knights*
　　　³　*gorgeous, exotic*

Finally, exhausted and delirious, Lear lies down and sleeps.

Is there any cause in nature that make these hard hearts?

"How can there be such men and women? we ask ourselves. How comes it that humanity can take such absolutely opposite forms? And, in particular, to what omission of elements which should be present in human nature, or, if there is no omission, to what distortion of these elements is it due that such beings as some of these come to exist? . . . In King Lear, this question is provoked again and again. And more, it seems to us that the author himself is asking this question."

A. C. Bradley, *Shakespearean Tragedy*, 1904

Lear is carried to safety

Just as Lear falls asleep, Gloucester rushes in. He has overheard, in the castle, that Lear is not simply to be left to wander at large: the talk is now of finding him and putting him to death.

Lear must be taken away from Gloucester's castle immediately; any delay will mean the death of the King and anyone found with him. Gloucester has secretly arranged transport for Lear, and he tells Kent to take him to Dover, where his supporters are gathered. Gloucester, Kent and the Fool carry off the sleeping King.

Edgar, left behind, reflects on the dreadful madness which has overtaken Lear, brought about by his daughters' cruelty. His own father's cruelty, in sentencing him to death, has distressed and frightened Edgar, but has not driven him to madness. He is determined to stay in his disguise as Poor Tom until the truth of his innocence emerges, and the accusations against him are seen to be unfounded:

Edgar   Mark the high noises,[1] and thyself bewray[2]
            When false opinion, whose wrong thoughts
                defile thee,
            In thy just proof repeals and reconciles thee.[3]

[1] *observe the discord amongst those in authority*
[2] *reveal yourself, abandon your disguise*
[3] *is forced, by proof of your innocence, to withdraw
     your sentence and allow you to be reconciled with
     your father*

Cornwall takes his revenge

III, vii

Cornwall tells Goneril to return at once to her husband, the Duke of Albany, and inform him of the latest developments. It is essential that the two rulers work together to repel the invasion from France. Cornwall instructs Edmund to accompany Goneril: he does not wish him to witness the revenge that is to befall his father, Gloucester, who has now been captured.

Oswald, Goneril's steward, reports that Gloucester has arranged for Lear to be taken to Dover. Lear is already on his way, accompanied by the remainder of his retinue of knights: of the original hundred, about thirty-five followers have remained loyal.

Gloucester is brought in to face the wrath of Cornwall and his wife Regan. The Duke orders his servants to bind the old man to a chair. Gloucester protests; they are guests at his castle, and should not mistreat him. Ignoring his complaints, Regan screams abuse at him and pulls violently at his beard.

Cornwall and Regan interrogate him fiercely, warning him that they already know of his support for the enemy. They demand to know why he has sent Lear to Dover, where he is beyond their reach. Gloucester has no choice but to admit his loyalty to the King:

Cornwall	Where hast thou sent the King?
Gloucester	To Dover.
Regan	Wherefore[1] to Dover? Wast thou not charg'd at peril -[2]
Cornwall	Wherefore to Dover? Let him answer that.
Gloucester	I am tied to th'stake, and I must stand the course.[3]
Regan	Wherefore to Dover?
Gloucester	Because I would not see

Thy cruel nails pluck out his poor old eyes;
Nor thy fierce sister in his anointed flesh
Rash[4] boarish fangs.

[1] *why*
[2] *ordered on pain of death (not to do anything to help Lear)*
[3] *suffer the onslaught, like a chained animal facing a pack (or 'course') of dogs*
[4] *jab, dig*

Gloucester realises that he will be punished, but his conso-lation, he says, is that he will eventually see Lear's cruel daugh-ters reap their rewards. Cornwall's response is immediate, brutal and horrifically apt:

Gloucester	. . . I shall see
	The winged[1] vengeance overtake such children.
Cornwall	See't shalt thou never. Fellows, hold the chair.
	Upon these eyes of thine I'll set my foot.

[1] *divine: swift*

He gouges Gloucester's eye out. Amid the old man's cries for help and screams of agony, Regan urges Cornwall to put his other eye out. One of Cornwall's servants intervenes, pleading with him to do no more. The Duke turns on him angrily, drawing his sword, and the two men fight.

Regan, furious at the servant's interference, grabs a sword and runs him through from behind, killing him instantly. Cornwall, injured in the fight, turns on Gloucester again, putting out his other eye.

. . . I must stand the course.

A few minutes' walk from the Globe Theatre, where many of Shakespeare's plays were first performed, was the Bear Garden, a large open-air arena. A German traveller of the time describes a visit:

"Without the city are some theatres, where English actors represent almost every day comedies and tragedies to very numerous audiences . . . There is still another place, built in the form of a theatre, which serves for the baiting of bears and bulls. They are fastened behind, and then worried by those great English dogs and mastiffs . . . To this entertainment there often follows that of whipping a blinded bear, which is performed by five or six men, standing in a circle with whips, which they exercise upon him without any mercy. He cannot escape from them because of his chains . . ."

Paul Hentzner, *Travels in England*, 1598

Gloucester learns the truth

Gloucester calls out for his son Edmund to come and revenge this monstrous act. Regan taunts him with the dreadful truth: it was Edmund who betrayed him, Edmund who revealed the existence of the incriminating letter.

In an instant Gloucester realises with horror what has happened. The letter that convinced him of Edgar's murderous intentions was a forgery. Edmund has deceived him all along; Edgar is innocent.

Cornwall and Regan leave, ordering Gloucester to be turned out of the castle. The body of the servant who died is to be thrown on the dunghill. Cornwall's injury is serious, and Regan supports him as they make their exit.

Cornwall's servants are stunned at what they have just witnessed. They are sure that such acts are bound to have terrible consequences; neither Cornwall nor Regan can escape retribution for long. They resolve to help Gloucester. First they will prepare a balm to apply to his wounded face, and then they will find someone to lead him. One of the servants has an idea. Someone who will easily be persuaded to lead Gloucester wherever he wishes is the mad but harmless vagrant who has been seen around the castle recently, Poor Tom.

Gloucester sets out on a journey

IV, i

Out on the open heath, Edgar is contemplating his situation. Buoyant and positive by nature, he reflects that his grim plight and his abject disguise are, in a sense, liberating; he has nothing to lose, owes nothing to anyone, and is confident that things can only get better. It is at this point that Edgar is shaken to the core by an appalling sight: it is his own father, blinded, his eyes bandaged, being led across the heath towards him.

Kindly but firmly, Gloucester asks the old man who is guiding him to leave him alone. The man protests:

Old Man	You cannot see your way.
Gloucester	I have no way, and therefore want no eyes; I stumbled when I saw.[1]

> [1]   *I did not see the truth when I had my eyesight*

The old man notices Poor Tom, and Gloucester realises that this is the same half-naked wretch that the King had befriended in last night's storm. The memory of the night's terrible events, as well as his misjudgement of his two sons, with its catastrophic results, has given Gloucester a bleak view of the world:

Gloucester	. . . As flies to wanton[1] boys, are we to th'Gods; They kill us for their sport.

> [1]   *wild, playful*

Gloucester asks the old man to fetch some clothes for Poor Tom, whom he intends to employ as a guide. Edgar, distressed to see his father reduced to such a state, finds it almost impossible to carry on as Poor Tom: but he feels he must stay in disguise until his innocence is established beyond doubt.

Gloucester approaches, and asks Poor Tom to lead him to Dover. He gives the beggar his purse, for which he has no further use. He will not miss it, he says, reflecting that he has always had more wealth than he needed; now, his suffering has led him to believe that riches should be spread more evenly.

Gloucester   Here, take this purse, thou whom the heav'ns'
                plagues
           Have humbled to all strokes:[1] that I am
                wretched
           Makes thee the happier: Heavens, deal so still![2]
           . . . So distribution should undo excess,[3]
           And each man have enough.

[1] *brought so low that you can bear anything without complaining*
[2] *let this always be so*
[3] *in this way, sharing would bring an end to excessive, unnecessary wealth*

Gloucester recalls that there is a high, steep cliff in Dover. He tells Poor Tom to guide him to the very edge of the cliff; from there, he will not need to be guided any further.

Goneril and her husband clash

IV, ii

Goneril, returning from Gloucester's castle, arrives back at her palace. She is accompanied by Edmund, now Earl of Gloucester. Her steward Oswald has been sent ahead to inform the Duke of Albany of the invasion from France.

Oswald, who has reported the news to Albany, comes out to greet Goneril as she arrives. He is baffled by Albany's response, he tells her. The Duke seemed to be completely unmoved by the news of the invasion: and told of Gloucester's treachery and Edmund's loyalty to Cornwall, he scolded Oswald for failing to see the truth. Goneril, who is becoming increasingly irritated by her husband's mildness and lack of aggression, realises that she will have to take the leading role in responding to the invasion.

Edmund must now return to the castle and help Cornwall with his military preparations. Before he goes, the intense sexual attraction that has grown between Goneril and Edmund becomes clear. She hints that, one way or another, her husband may soon be disposed of:

Goneril   . . . ere long you are like to hear,
            If you dare venture in your own behalf,[1]
            A mistress's command.

> [1] *if you have the courage to act in your own interests*

She kisses Edmund passionately. As he leaves, she reflects on the difference between the two men: Edmund, who arouses her deepest emotions, and Albany, for whom she feels nothing but scorn.

Albany now comes out to meet Goneril. His usual calmness

gives way as he reproaches her angrily for her cruelty towards her father:

Albany   What have you done?
            Tigers, not daughters, what have you perform'd?
            A father, and a gracious aged man,
            Whose reverence even the head-lugg'd[1] bear
                would lick,
            Most barbarous, most degenerate! have you
                madded.
            . . . If that the heavens do not their visible
                spirits
            Send quickly down to tame these vilde
                offences,[2]
            It will come,
            Humanity must perforce prey on itself,
            Like monsters of the deep.

[1] *enraged, baited by being tugged around by the head*
[2] *avenge these violent acts*

Goneril is contemptuous of her husband's moralising. There is urgent business in hand, she retorts: France has invaded, and the Duke has done nothing.

> "... as any socio-biologist knows, nature is not constructed solely of egotism. The survival of a species depends also upon altruism exercised within the group, generally by parents in favour of their young, but also by individuals in favour of the group. Albany recoils from the savage ethos in which his wife lives, foreseeing both her own destruction and that of the universe itself as a consequence of unbridled self-interest."
>
> Germaine Greer, *Shakespeare*, 1986

A fateful message

In the midst of the furious argument between Goneril and her husband, a messenger enters. The Duke of Cornwall has just died.

The messenger describes the circumstances of Cornwall's death: he received the fatal wound when his servant, unable to stand by while his master put out Gloucester's eyes, challenged him. Albany is appalled to hear of the punishment inflicted on the old Earl. The only consolation is that vengeance has come so swiftly to the perpetrator.

Goneril's reaction to the news is in sharp contrast to her husband's. Her first thought is that Cornwall's death is to her advantage; rule over the entire kingdom is now a distinct possibility. However, she cannot rid herself of the hateful image in her mind of her sister, now a widow, and Edmund, together in Gloucester's castle. The ambitious Edmund, in his unceasing quest for power, wealth and land, may be tempted to marry Regan. The idea is unbearable: it must be prevented from happening at all costs.

Lear and Cordelia are still apart

IV, iii

In Dover, the disguised Kent has caught up with the gentle-man whom he earlier dispatched to see Cordelia. The man has delivered a letter in which Kent described how Lear was shut out by Goneril and Regan, and left to wander through the stormy night.

Kent asks the gentleman how Cordelia reacted on reading of her sisters' cruelty. She was distressed rather than angry, he replies:

Kent   O! then it mov'd her.
Gentleman   Not to a rage; patience and sorrow strove
                 Who should express her goodliest.[1] You have
                     seen
                 Sunshine and rain at once; her smiles and tears
                 Were like, a better way . . .[2]

> [1] *competed with each other in displaying her beauty*
> [2] *were similar, but even more graceful*

By now Lear is also in Dover, but he has not been reunited with Cordelia. Kent explains that he has lucid moments, when his sanity seems to return, but he refuses all appeals to join his loyal daughter. The reason, he says, is Lear's unbearable sense of guilt at how he treated her:

Kent   A sovereign shame so elbows him:[1] his own
            unkindness,
        That stripp'd her from his benediction, turn'd
            her
        To foreign casualties,[2] gave her dear rights
        To his dog-hearted daughters, these things sting
        His mind so venomously that burning shame
        Detains him from Cordelia.

[1] *holds him back*
[2] *chances, uncertainties*

Cordelia prepares for battle

IV, iv

Cordelia is standing at the head of the invading army. She has just heard news of her father: he has been seen wandering, deranged, through the fields, singing and shouting, wearing a crown of weeds and nettles. She sends out a search party at once to bring him to her.

Alarmed at Lear's condition, she asks the doctor accompanying her what can be done to help; she would give anything, she tells him, for her father to be cured. All that medicine can do, he replies, is help him to rest. Given a long enough period of tranquillity, Lear should recover naturally:

Cordelia	What can man's wisdom[1]
	In the restoring his bereaved sense?
	He that helps him take all my outward worth.[2]
Doctor	There is means, Madam;
	Our foster-nurse of nature is repose,
	The which he lacks; that to provoke in him,
	Are many simples operative,[3] whose power
	Will close the eye of anguish.
Cordelia	All bless'd secrets,
	All you unpublish'd virtues of the earth,[4]
	Spring with my tears! be aidant and remediate
	In the good man's distress!

[1] *what can human knowledge achieve*
[2] *material wealth*
[3] *effective medicinal herbs*
[4] *healing plants and herbs, as yet unknown*

News arrives that the British troops of Cornwall and Albany are approaching. Cordelia is unshaken: the movements of the opposing armies have been monitored closely, and her troops are prepared.

Although the invading force has come from France, the King of France himself is not present. It was on Cordelia's insistence that he provided troops, and the aim of the invasion is to restore the King, not to enlarge the territory of France:

Cordelia	No blown[1] ambition doth our arms incite,
	But love, dear love, and our ag'd father's right.

[1] *proud, grandiose*

"Cordelia's tenderness is rooted in the same strength that enabled her to reject Lear's misconceived demands . . . Her love is of a kind that, confronted with a real demand, does not bargain or make conditions; it is freely given, and it represents an absolute of human experience that can stand against the full shock of disillusion."

L. C. Knights, *King Lear and the Great Tragedies*, 1955

Regan distrusts her sister

IV, v

Regan is still in Gloucester's castle, from which the old, blinded Earl was ejected. Goneril's messenger Oswald arrives, and confirms that Albany's army has been mobilised, although Goneril has been far more enthusiastic than her husband in preparing for war. Oswald has come with a letter from Goneril for Edmund.

Regan, like her sister, has become infatuated with Edmund, and intends to marry him. Edmund has declared his love for her, but she does not trust him. She tries to persuade Oswald to describe the contents of Goneril's note, tormented by the thought that Goneril and Edmund may secretly be exchanging love-letters; but Oswald diplomatically refuses.

Edmund has gone to observe the strength of the invading army, she says, and it would be foolhardy to follow him with the letter; but Oswald insists that he must do his duty. Finally, she pleads with him to hand over the letter so that she can open it. When she sees that he will not, she comes out, in desperation, with the truth: she knows that Goneril does not love her husband, and she has noticed her casting amorous, knowing glances in Edmund's direction.

Regan instructs Oswald to pass a clear message on to his mistress. It is more fitting for Regan, as a widow, to consort with Edmund: Goneril must come to her senses and leave him alone.

Regan is unhappy, in retrospect, that Gloucester was allowed to live following his punishment. She fears that he will arouse sympathy for the King's side, and resentment against Regan and the British forces, wherever he goes. She hints that it will be greatly to Oswald's advantage if he can track down the old man and put him to death. Oswald takes the hint at once:

Regan	If you do chance to hear of that blind traitor,
	Preferment[1] falls on him that cuts him off.[2]
Oswald	Would I could meet him, Madam: I should show
	What party I do follow.

[1] *favour, promotion*
[2] *ends his life*

Gloucester regains the will to live

IV, vi

Edgar continues to lead his blind father on the long journey to Dover. He has been supplied with clothing, and is no longer ranting madly as he had done earlier. Gloucester notices a difference in his speech, but Edgar still does not reveal his true identity.

Realising that he intends to commit suicide by throwing himself off Dover cliff, Edgar is determined to cure his father of his deep sense of despair. They are now a short distance away from Dover, but Edgar tells his father that they are already approaching the cliff. Pretending to lead Gloucester to the edge, Edgar describes the frightening view over the precipice:

Edgar   Come on, sir; here's the place: stand still. How
              fearful
           And dizzy 'tis to cast one's eyes so low!
           The crows and choughs[1] that wing the midway
              air
           Show scarce so gross as beetles . . .

           [1] *jackdaws*

Gloucester asks to be taken to the very edge of the cliff, and Edgar leads him forward. Gloucester pulls out a purse which has been hidden in his clothing; it contains a precious jewel, he says, giving it to Poor Tom as a reward for guiding him on the long journey.

The old man says a final, solemn prayer to the gods. He cannot face life any longer, he says: suicide may be wrong, but even if he were not to kill himself he would soon die of misery and regret. He says farewell to Poor Tom, and asks for the blessing of the gods on his wronged son Edgar. Finally he throws himself forward. Although Gloucester falls harmlessly to the ground, Edgar comes immediately to his side, fearing that his father may simply have died through despair: but he is still alive.

Addressing his father, Edgar now changes his accent once again. Standing on the beach at the foot of the cliff, he tells him, he has just seen Gloucester fall hundreds of feet from the cliff top; it is nothing short of a miracle that he is still alive.

> *"The blind Gloucester falls over on the empty stage. His suicidal leap is tragic... But the pantomime performed by actors on the stage is grotesque, and has something of a circus about it. The blind Gloucester who has climbed a non-existent height and fallen over on flat boards, is a clown. A philosophical buffoonery has been performed, of the sort found in modern theatre."*
>
> Jan Kott, *Shakespeare Our Contemporary*, 1965

Gloucester's first reaction is frustration that he has not succeeded in ending his life. Edgar tells him that, from down on the beach, where they are now, he saw a strange, sinister creature next to Gloucester before he fell. The urge to commit suicide must have been instilled into him by this fiend: and the gods, taking pity on him, have allowed him to survive his deadly jump over the cliff's edge.

Edgar   As I stood here below methought his eyes
         Were two full moons; he had a thousand noses,
         Horns whelk'd[1] and wav'd like the enridged sea:
         It was some fiend; therefore, thou happy father,
         Think that the clearest[2] Gods, who make them
             honours
         Of men's impossibilities,[3] have preserved thee.

[1] *twisted, spiral*
[2] *pure, direct, clear-sighted*
[3] *who win our reverence by carrying out acts that*
    appear to us impossible

Gloucester realises that Poor Tom, who had often babbled wildly about the 'foul fiend', was indeed possessed by an evil spirit. The gods do not intend him to die yet: he resolves to stay alive and bear his suffering patiently until his time comes.

"Il gît en votre volonté, non au nombre des ans, que vous ayez assez vécu."

Whether you have lived long enough depends on your own will, not on the number of your years.

Michel de Montaigne, *Essais*, 1588

Lear is found

Just as Edgar has succeeded in soothing his father's despondency, another image of human suffering appears before him, a mad, raving, bizarrely dressed old man, with wild flowers festooned about his head. It is King Lear. Gloucester recognises his voice:

Gloucester	The trick of that voice I do well remember:
	Is't not the King?
Lear	Ay, every inch a king:
	When I do stare, see how the subject quakes.

In his madness, Lear has become obsessed with sexuality, hypocrisy and injustice. He sees the world as rife with corruption: dark, evil forces are at work everywhere, hidden under the veneer of civilised behaviour. Noticing Gloucester, whose illegitimate son Edmund he believes, misguidedly, to have shown great loyalty, he imagines himself passing judgement:

Lear	I pardon that man's life. What was thy cause?[1]
	Adultery?
	Thou shalt not die: die for adultery! No:
	The wren goes to't, and the small gilded fly
	Does lecher[2] in my sight.
	Let copulation thrive; for Gloucester's bastard
	son
	Was kinder to his father than my daughters
	Got[3] 'tween the lawful sheets.

[1] *charge*
[2] *copulate*
[3] *conceived*

Lear is convinced that the worst sinners are those in authority, and those who are protected by their wealth and status. It is the poor and the defenceless who suffer at the hands of justice: they are the innocent ones, says Lear, and as King he will take their side and silence their accusers. He turns to the blinded Gloucester again. Suffering is the natural state of humanity, he explains:

Lear   ... I know thee well enough; thy name is
                Gloucester;
            Thou must be patient; we came crying
                hither ...[1]
            When we are born, we cry that we are come
            To this great stage of fools.

[1] into this world

Lear's thoughts then veer off in another direction as he imagines taking violent revenge on his persecutors. It is at this point that a group of soldiers from the search party sent out by Cordelia enters. They try to persuade Lear to go with them. Lear, thinking that they intend to arrest and perhaps kill him, runs off, with the soldiers in pursuit.

> "From October 1810 until April 1820, King Lear was not acted on any stage in London; since George III, like Lear, was old and mad and the king of England, any performance of the play would inevitably have suggested uncomfortable parallels with the living royal family."
>
> Gary Taylor, *Reinventing Shakespeare*, 1990

A conspiracy is revealed

Edgar stops a member of the search party for a moment. He wants to establish the whereabouts of the advancing army of Cornwall and Albany. He is told that the army is no more than a few hours from Dover.

Gloucester is curious to know more about this stranger, who

found him at the foot of the cliff and who is now guiding him. Edgar still does not reveal his true identity. He tells Gloucester that he is someone who, having experienced misfortune himself, is ready to show sympathy to others. He will find him somewhere to stay, he promises, and they continue on their way.

Oswald, who is taking Goneril's letter to Edmund, now comes across the two men. He is delighted to have chanced upon the old Earl of Gloucester, remembering Regan's promise that his executioner would be treated generously:

Oswald   A proclaim'd[1] prize! Most happy!
That eyeless head of thine was first fram'd flesh[2]
To raise my fortunes. Thou old unhappy traitor,
Briefly thyself remember:[3] the sword is out
That must destroy thee.

[1] *with a price on his head*
[2] *created*
[3] *think of your sins, in preparation for death*

Gloucester, unafraid and ready to welcome death, makes no attempt to escape. However, his son steps forward to defend him. Speaking in a broad dialect in case Oswald recognises him, he warns the messenger to leave them alone. Angered by his intervention, Oswald turns on Edgar and attacks him.

Armed only with a wooden stave against Oswald's sword, Edgar manages to hold the messenger off, and eventually deals him a fatal blow. As he dies, Oswald reveals that he is carrying a letter for Edmund, Earl of Gloucester: it must be delivered.

Edgar looks through the messenger's pockets and finds the letter. He decides, hesitantly, to read it, and breaks the seal.

Edgar   . . . Leave, gentle wax; and, manners, blame us
                   not:
               To know our enemies' minds, we rip their
                   hearts;
               Their papers[1] is more lawful.

     [1] *to rip open their letters*

He is shocked by the contents of the letter:

*Let our reciprocal vows be remembered. You have
many opportunities to cut him off;[1] if your will want
not,[2] time and place will be fruitfully offer'd. There
is nothing done if he return the conqueror;[3] then I am
the prisoner, and his bed my gaol; from the loathed
warmth whereof deliver me, and supply the place for
your labour.*
               Your wife, so I would say -
                   Affectionate servant,
                       GONERIL.

     [1] *end his life*
     [2] *if you are sufficiently determined*
     [3] *even if he defeats the invading army*

The letter is a reminder to Edmund to carry out his promise,
and murder her husband, the Duke of Albany. Edgar knows Albany to be a good man, even though he is bound to oppose the
invasion from France, and decides that he must be made aware
of the plot against his life. When the time is right, Edgar plans
to make his way to the British lines: first, he will lead his father
to some lodgings, where he can find rest, safety and compan-
ionship.

Lear and Cordelia are reunited

IV, vii

The Earl of Kent has now joined Cordelia in the French camp at Dover. She thanks him wholeheartedly for the care and loyalty he has shown to Lear. Kent is still in the disguise that he put on long ago, when he was banished by the King: he asks Cordelia to keep the secret of his true identity until he decides to reveal, publicly, who he is.

Lear, led back to Cordelia's camp by the soldiers who found him, has been sleeping heavily. The doctor decides that he can now be woken, and he is carried in on a chair. The doctor believes that Lear's prospects of recovery from his state of mental disturbance are good. He calls for music to be played, to rouse the King gently from sleep.

Cordelia kisses her father, and he begins to regain consciousness. His first thought is that he is in hell, and the sight of Cordelia, who seems to him a heavenly spirit, perplexes him:

Lear	You do me wrong to take me out o'th'grave;
	Thou art a soul in bliss; but I am bound
	Upon a wheel of fire, that mine own tears
	Do scald like molten lead.

"The old Lear died in the storm. The new Lear is born in the scene in which he is reunited with Cordelia. His madness marked the end of the wilful, egotistical monarch. He is resurrected as a fully human being . . . the awakening into life is a painful process."

Kenneth Muir, Introduction to the Arden Shakespeare edition of *King Lear*, 1972

As he becomes wider awake, he gradually grows aware of himself and his surroundings. He realises that he is in an unfamiliar place: he tries to remember how he came to be where he is, but cannot. However, he dimly recalls events to do with his three daughters; he recognises Cordelia, and knows that she has cause to be displeased with him.

Cordelia is overjoyed that he remembers her, and her forgiveness is immediate and unconditional:

Lear	Do not laugh at me;
	For, as I am a man, I think this lady
	To be my child Cordelia.
Cordelia	And so I am, I am.
Lear	Be your tears wet? Yes, faith. I pray, weep not:
	If you have poison for me, I will drink it.
	I know you do not love me; for your sisters
	Have, as I do remember, done me wrong:
	You have some cause, they have not.
Cordelia	No cause, no cause.

The doctor decides that Lear's mental stability is returning, but that further rest is needed. Above all, he must not yet be made to talk or think about the half-remembered events that brought about the turmoil in his mind.

When Cordelia has led her father out, one of the King's supporters asks Kent about the Duke of Cornwall. Kent confirms that the Duke has died from his injuries: his army is now under the command of Edmund. The man mentions that the Earl of Kent and Gloucester's other son Edgar are both reported to be in Germany. The disguised Kent replies, laconically, that rumours can never be trusted.

Discord in the British camp

V, i

The British have set up camp near Dover, in readiness for battle with the invading force from France. The two sections of the
British army are led by Edmund and the Duke of Albany. Edmund is becoming impatient with his senior partner, who seems
unenthusiastic and indecisive in his preparation for war against
the King's supporters.

Regan takes Edmund aside. Goneril's messenger Oswald
seems to have come to grief, she says. On the subject of Goneril,
she forces herself to ask the question which has been torment-
ing her. Edmund's answers are evasive:

Regan	. . . Tell me, but truly, but then speak the truth,
	Do you not love my sister?
Edmund	In honour'd love.
Regan	But have you never found my brother's way
	To the forfended place?[1]
Edmund	That thought abuses you.[2]

[1] *the forbidden place, Goneril's bed*
[2] *deceives you: is unworthy of you*

Besides, Edmund points out, Goneril is married; and to the
respected Duke of Albany, the most important man in Britain.
Regan, infatuated with Edmund but distrustful of him, is not
reassured. She begs him to stay away from her sister.

Albany and Goneril now arrive at the camp with their troops.
Like her sister, Goneril is preoccupied with her relationship with
Edmund:

Goneril   [*aside*] I had rather lose the battle than that
                sister
            Should loosen him and me.

Albany addresses Edmund. He has profound misgivings over the forthcoming conflict. An invasion by France is clearly a serious matter: however, the invading forces now include many British subjects who have justifiable grievances, and their main aim is to express their dissatisfaction, and to show support for Lear, not to occupy British territory. Far from being opposed to Lear and Cordelia, Albany sympathises with them.

Edmund, scornful of Albany's reluctance, puts on an air of appreciative respect. Goneril and Regan, equally, have no time for Albany's moral niceties: they urge him to prepare for war immediately, and the four of them leave for Albany's tent, where the commanding officers are to be consulted.

Just as Albany is going out, a man dressed in threadbare clothes approaches him and hands him a letter. It is Edgar, still in disguise. The letter, which he found on Oswald's body, proves beyond doubt that Goneril and Edmund are conspiring to take Albany's life. Before Albany reads the letter, Edgar asks him to agree that, if he is victorious in the approaching battle, he will order a trumpet to be sounded: a warrior will then appear, Edgar promises, to vouch that the letter is genuine. Edgar then hurries away.

Edmund comes back, urging Albany to prepare his troops for battle. The invading army is now in sight.

> *"Edmund is beautiful as an animal, physically a paragon of animals, with an animal's lithe grace, a cat's heartless skill in tormenting the weak . . . He is playing a game. And he has an impudent charm of conscious superiority and sex-attraction."*
>
> G. Wilson Knight, *The Wheel of Fire*, 1930

Edmund plans his future

As Albany goes to join the council of war, Edmund reflects, with cynical amusement, on the situation with Goneril and Regan:

Edmund   To both these sisters have I sworn my love;
Each jealous[1] of the other, as the stung
Are of the adder. Which of them shall I take?
Both? one? or neither? Neither can be enjoy'd
If both remain alive . . .

[1] *suspicious, wary*

Although Albany's presence will be needed in the impending battle, Edmund is relying on Goneril to help him do away with the Duke when the fighting is over. It is more than likely that jealousy will provoke one of the sisters to kill the other: Edmund intends to marry the survivor. Whichever sister it is, he will thereby become the sole and absolute ruler of Britain.

The survival of Lear and Cordelia would pose a serious obstacle to his ambition. Albany may talk of showing them mercy, but Edmund's plans demand an altogether more ruthless approach.

Gloucester's journey continues

V, ii

Edgar, still hiding his true identity, continues to guide and care for his father. At the moment they are close to the point where the battle is to take place. The invading army, with Lear and Cordelia at its head, is advancing towards the British camp. Edgar leads his father to the shade of a tree, and goes to observe the conflict.

When Edgar returns, he brings bad news. The armies of Albany and Edmund have been victorious: the troops loyal to the King have been defeated, and Lear and Cordelia taken prisoner.

They must escape quickly, Edgar tells his father. If captured by the British, Gloucester would certainly be put to death. Gloucester, weary and dejected, decides that he may as well stay where he is. Edgar urges him on. He must die when he is ready, and not at someone else's whim:

Gloucester	No further, sir; a man may rot[1] even here.
Edgar	What! in ill thoughts again? Men must endure Their going hence even as their coming hither: Ripeness[2] is all.

[1] *die, decay*
[2] *readiness, preparedness*

Gloucester allows himself to be led away to safety.

"Although affliction cometh not forth of the dust, neither doth trouble spring out of the ground; Yet man is born unto trouble, as the sparks fly upward . . . Behold, happy is the man whom God correcteth: therefore despise not thou the chastening of the Almighty: for He maketh sore, and bindeth up: He woundeth, and His hands make whole . . . Thou shalt come to thy grave in a full age, like as a shock of corn cometh in his season."

The Book of Job, King James Bible, 1611

Lear renounces the world

V, iii

Edmund leads his troops victoriously back to the British camp.
Lear and Cordelia are brought in as prisoners. Edmund announces
that they must be guarded carefully until those with greater authority - such as the Duke of Albany - pass judgement on them.

Cordelia tells her father that she can face the prospect of
prison with equanimity, but is distressed on his behalf:

Cordelia   We are not the first
            Who, with best meaning,[1] have incurr'd the
                worst.
            For thee, oppressed King, I am cast down;
            Myself could else out-frown false Fortune's
                frown.

    [1] intentions

But Lear too is unafraid of captivity. In fact, as long as he
is with Cordelia, it will be a pleasure to be shut out of the life
of the court, rather than be part of it:

Lear   Come, let's away to prison;
We two alone will sing like birds i'th'cage . . .
And pray, and sing, and tell old tales, and
      laugh
At gilded butterflies, and hear poor rogues
Talk of court news; and we'll talk with them
      too,
Who loses and who wins; who's in, who's
      out . . .
                              . . . and we'll wear out,[1]
In a wall'd prison, packs and sects of great ones
That ebb and flow by th'moon.[2]

[1] *outlast*
[2] *those in high office, who organise themselves into
    various factions and parties, whose good fortune
    never lasts long*

Lear comforts Cordelia: Goneril, Regan and the rest of them
will eventually come to grief, he tells her, while the two of them
will live simply and happily together in prison.

---

*"Only at the end does Lear realise, as a sane man, that power,
revenge, and victory are not worth while. But by the time he
makes this discovery, it is too late . . ."*

George Orwell, *Lear, Tolstoy, and the Fool,* 1947

Edmund delegates an important task

Edmund orders the prisoners to be taken away. He then takes one of his captains to one side. Despite his earlier announcement that Lear and Cordelia were to be sentenced by those in authority, he has already decided on their fate: but he needs help in carrying out his plan.

Handing the officer a sealed order, Edmund tells him that there is an important task that needs to be carried out. The officer has already gained promotion under Edmund's patronage: if he performs this duty, his fortunes will reach new heights. They have been at war, says Edmund, and this is not the time to feel pity or uncertainty. He requires absolute commitment from his officer, and he receives it:

Edmund	One step I have advanc'd thee; if thou dost As this[1] instructs thee, thou dost make thy way To noble fortunes; know thou this, that men Are as the time is; to be tender-minded Does not become a sword;[2] thy great employment Will not bear question;[3] either say thou'lt do't, Or thrive by other means.
Officer	I'll do't, my Lord.

[1] *this sealed order*
[2] *is not fitting for a soldier*
[3] *there can be no discussion about the rights and wrongs of this important task*

The captain takes Edmund's note and leaves, determined to carry out his duty.

Regan makes a desperate bid

Albany now returns to the camp, accompanied by Goneril and Regan. He compliments Edmund on the military prowess he has shown in the day's action. He then asks, diplomatically but firmly, for Edmund to hand over the prisoners he has taken during the battle: as ruler, the Duke wishes to look at their cases and pass judgement accordingly.

Edmund's response is lengthy and evasive. It is best for the King and Cordelia to be kept under guard and out of sight for a while, he says: whenever they are seen in public, they are likely to arouse sympathy, even among the conscripts in the British forces. Besides, in the present circumstances, just after a fierce battle in which many lives have been lost, it is unlikely that the two prisoners would receive a fair trial.

The Duke is unimpressed by his arguments. Edmund does not have the authority to make such decisions, he tells him:

Edmund	. . . The question of Cordelia and her father
	Requires a fitter place.
Albany	Sir, by your patience,
	I hold you but a subject of this war,
	Not as a brother.[1]

> [1] *a subordinate, not an equal*

Regan now breaks in: whatever Albany may say, she, as widow of the Duke of Cornwall, considers Edmund to be Albany's equal. She has put him in command of of her army and, in effect, he has acted in the capacity of the late Duke. Goneril interrupts furiously: it is Edmund's own worth that makes him Albany's equal, not any titles that Regan may wish to bestow on him.

In the acrimonious argument that follows, Regan, who is suffering from a sudden bout of sickness, makes an impetuous declaration to Edmund:

Regan   General,
      Take thou my soldiers, prisoners, patrimony;[1]
      Dispose of them, of me; the walls are thine;[2]
      Witness the world, that I create thee here
      My lord and master.

> [1] *inheritance, estate*
> [2] *you have conquered my heart, and won my love*

Goneril is aghast at her sister's shameless attempt to drag Edmund into marriage. Albany points out that she can do nothing to prevent it.

Edmund, who has been silent throughout these angry exchanges, now turns on Albany, and tells him that he too is powerless to prevent his marriage; if he wishes, he will marry Regan and become, in the process, ruler of half of Britain.

> *"The two daughters, by their actions, by what they say, and by the imagery of beasts of prey so consistently associated with them, represent a ferocious animality."*
>
> L. C. Knights, *King Lear and the Great Tragedies*, 1955

Edmund prepares to defend himself

As the arguments build up to an angry climax, Albany calls for silence. He makes a dramatic announcement:

Albany   Stay yet; hear reason. Edmund, I arrest thee
                     On capital[1] treason; and, in thy attaint,[2]
                     This gilded serpent.[3]

       [1] *punishable by death*
       [2] *sharing in the treason of which I accuse you*
       [3] *Goneril*

Albany knows, from the letter handed to him before the battle, that Edmund and Goneril are plotting to take his life. He does not reveal the existence of the letter, but he tells Regan, sardonically, that her marriage cannot go ahead; Edmund has already come to an agreement with his wife. Goneril is exasperated by her husband's dry, enigmatic comments:

Albany   For your claim, fair sister,
                     I bar it in the interest of my wife;
                     'Tis she is sub-contracted to this lord,
                     And I, her husband, contradict your banes.[1]
                     If you will marry, make your loves to me,
                     My lady is bespoke.[2]
Goneril   An interlude![3]

       [1] *disallow your announced intention to marry*
       [2] *already pledged (to Edmund)*
       [3] *a play, entertainment*

Becoming serious again, Albany turns to Edmund and repeats his accusation of treason. Albany remembers what the anonymous bearer of the incriminating letter had said. If the British were victorious, a trumpet should be sounded: a warrior would then arrive, he promised, to confront Edmund.

Albany intends to sound the trumpet, but regardless of the stranger's promise he is ready to face up to Edmund himself. He throws down his glove: if no-one else appears, Albany will challenge Edmund to fight, in single combat, to the death. Edmund immediately throws down his own glove in response: he is ready to take on anyone in defence of his honour.

Albany calls for a herald, so that Edmund's accuser can be officially summoned to come forward. As the herald approaches, it becomes clear that Regan's illness is becoming more serious, and she is led away. Goneril is pleased; the poison she has administered is taking effect.

The herald then makes the official proclamation: anyone who maintains that Edmund is a traitor must come forward, armed and ready to fight, by the third note of the trumpet. The trumpet sounds. No-one comes forward.

Edmund's accuser appears

The trumpet sounds again, and again there is no response. The trumpet sounds a third and final time. An answering trumpet-call is heard: the trumpeter enters, followed by an armed warrior.

The warrior is Edgar. Masked by his armour, he remains unrecognised, and refuses to say who he is:

Herald   What are you?
          Your name? your quality? and why you answer
          This present summons?
Edgar   Know, my name is lost;
          By treason's tooth bare-gnawn,[1] and canker-bit:[2]
          Yet I am noble as the adversary
          I come to cope.[3]

[1]   *eaten away to nothing*
[2]   *withered, ragged*
[3]   *challenge*

> *". . . there is no sense of divine action. It is Edgar's trumpet, symbol of natural judgement, that summons Edmund to account at the end, sounding through the Lear mist from which right and wrong at this moment emerge distinct."*
>
> G. Wilson Knight, *The Wheel of Fire*, 1930

Edgar tells Edmund to draw his sword, and denounces him as a traitor:

Edgar   . . . Maugre[1] thy strength, place,[2] youth, and
                 eminence,
             Despite thy victor sword and fire-new[3] fortune,
             Thy valour and thy heart, thou art a traitor,
             False to thy gods, thy brother, and thy father,
             Conspirant 'gainst this high illustrious
                 prince . . .

[1] *in spite of*
[2] *rank, status*
[3] *brand new, straight from the smith's furnace*

The stranger has not given his name and position. As Edmund points out, he is not obliged to take on an unknown opponent; he is only required to respond to a challenge from one of equal rank to himself. Nevertheless, says Edmund, the combat must go ahead, and the stranger must die for the hateful, slanderous accusations he has made. The two men cross swords and fight.

Vengeance

In the ensuing combat, Edmund falls to the ground, mortally wounded. Goneril cries out, distraught: Edmund has been tricked into fighting an unknown opponent, she claims, and the stranger's victory is worthless.

At this point Albany produces the letter, sent by Goneril but never delivered, in which the plot to murder the Duke is revealed. Goneril tries to snatch the letter from him, but fails. In desperation, she claims that she is above the law: then she storms out, refusing to answer any questions.

Edmund, his strength flagging, admits that the accusations made by the Duke and by the anonymous warrior are true. He asks his opponent to reveal who he is. For the first time since he was forced to flee from his father's castle, taking the disguise of a poor, mad beggar, Edgar publicly reclaims his true identity:

Edgar   My name is Edgar, and thy father's son.
              The Gods are just, and of our pleasant[1] vices
              Make instruments to plague us;
              The dark and vicious[2] place where thee he got[3]
              Cost him his eyes.

              [1] *pleasurable*
              [2] *sinful, adulterous*
              [3] *fathered*

Edgar describes how he has guided and protected the blind, aged Gloucester. He kept his identity secret from his father, he says, until just before his encounter with Edmund. When Gloucester realised that the man who had been caring for him for so long was his beloved son Edgar, whom he had wrongly accused of disloyalty, he was overwhelmed with emotion.

Father and son were at last reconciled; but for Gloucester,

racked with suffering and regret for so long, the happiness of the reunion also marked the time for his release, serene and ready, into death:

Edgar   . . . his flaw'd heart,
                    Alack, too weak the conflict to support!
                    'Twixt two extremes of passion, joy and grief,
                    Burst smilingly.

While Edgar was grieving over his dead father, Kent had approached. On discovering Edgar's true identity, and finding Gloucester dead, Kent was overcome with grief, and seemed on the verge of death himself. It was at this point, Edgar says, that the trumpet sounded, and he had come forward to face Edmund.

As Edgar is describing Kent's loyal service to the King, an attendant rushes in, carrying a bloodstained knife. Goneril has killed herself. Before dying, she confessed to having poisoned Regan, who is now also dead. Edmund, by now nearing death, remarks grimly that the three of them will soon be united:

Edmund   I was contracted[1] to them both: all three
                Now marry in an instant.

                    [1] *promised, betrothed*

The bodies of the two sisters are brought in.

Edmund has a change of heart

The Earl of Kent enters. He too, like Edgar, has abandoned his disguise. Sensing that his own end is near, he has come for a final reunion with his old master, the King.

Albany is reminded, with a shock, that Lear and Cordelia

are still imprisoned, and possibly in danger. He commands Edmund to tell him where they are being held. Edmund decides that, after all his deceit and treachery, he will try to do something to make amends. He tells the truth: Lear and Cordelia are imprisoned in a nearby castle, and he has sent one of his captains to execute them. Cordelia is to be killed first. The captain has been ordered to hang her and make it appear that she has committed suicide.

An officer is dispatched to the castle at once to save the King and his daughter. Taking Edmund's sword as proof that their lives are to be spared, the officer races off to stop the captain from carrying out his orders.

Lear's suffering comes to an end

It is too late.

A few moments after the officer has been dispatched, Lear himself comes into the camp. He is carrying Cordelia's lifeless body in his arms. She has been hanged. In the devastated silence that surrounds him, Lear cries out in anguish:

Lear   Howl, howl, howl! O! you are men of stones:[1]
            Had I your tongues and eyes, I'd use them so
            That heaven's vault should crack. She's gone for
                ever.
            I know when one is dead, and when one lives;
            She's dead as earth.

            [1] *hard-hearted, unfeeling*

Lear's fragile sanity, not long recovered, starts to crumble again under this new burden of grief, and he tries to persuade himself that Cordelia is still alive. It emerges that, in his rage, he overpowered and killed Edmund's captain:

Lear   Cordelia, Cordelia! stay a little. Ha!
            What is't thou say'st? Her voice was ever soft,
            Gentle and low, an excellent thing in woman.
            I kill'd the slave that was a-hanging thee.

Kent approaches Lear and tries to explain that, since his banishment, he has remained constantly at his side, in disguise: but Lear's eyesight, his memory and his reason are all failing, and Kent's words are wasted.

A messenger comes in to report that Edmund, who was carried out a few minutes ago, has died. In the present atmosphere of bleak despair, the news causes no shock or grief.

Albany says that everything possible will be done to comfort Lear. Moreover, he announces solemnly, all his power is to be handed over; Lear is King of Britain once more. Lear, however, is nearing the end, his body and mind both racked beyond endurance. He approaches Cordelia's corpse once again:

Lear   Why should a dog, a horse, a rat, have life,
            And thou no breath at all? Thou'lt come no
                more,
            Never, never, never, never, never!
                    . . . Look on her, look, her lips,
            Look there, look there!

Convinced that he sees signs of life in his dead daughter's face, Lear is overcome with joy. It is in this redeeming, ecstatic flood of emotion that he dies.

Just as the reconciliation of Lear and Cordelia is one of the most moving moments in English drama, Cordelia's death is surely one of the saddest.

In 1681, the poet Nahum Tate wrote an adaptation of *King Lear* in which Shakespeare's devastating final scene was replaced by a happy ending, with both Lear and Cordelia surviving. The adaptation was a great success: although the original play was still read and studied, it was to be nearly two hundred years before Shakespeare's *King Lear*, rather than Tate's, was regularly performed on stage.

Tate's play, now regarded as a museum-piece, is generally condemned as lightweight and sentimental. Nevertheless, a performance of Shakespeare's harsh, uncompromising masterpiece remains a harrowing experience for present-day audiences.

Edgar looks cautiously to the future

Edgar, seeing Lear fall, rushes to his side and tries to revive him. Kent gently dissuades Edgar: life for Lear can now hold nothing but pain.

Albany turns to Kent and Edgar. As his friends, and as loyal followers of the King, he asks the two of them to rule over Britain and restore harmony to the strife-torn nation. The old Earl of Kent declines; exhausted and dispirited, he feels that he will soon be following his master to the grave.

The government of Britain, then, falls on Edgar's shoulders. Despite his youth, resilience, and optimism, he too has been profoundly shaken by recent events. In place of flattery and de-

ception, which enable those with evil intentions to flourish, he
calls for sincerity, honesty and openness:

Edgar	The weight of this sad time we must obey;[1]
	Speak what we feel, not what we ought to say.
	The oldest hath borne most: we that are young
	Shall never see so much, nor live so long.

[1] *submit to, accept*

The sadness of the present time must be felt, and acknowl-
edged; it must be expressed; and its lessons must be learnt. The
bodies of the King and his three daughters are carried solemnly
away.

---

*"Shakespeare did not assemble all the varied materials of this
mighty play to leave us, at the end, with a capsule of facile
pessimism. In this story of a great offence, expiated by a great
suffering, we end at a higher point than we began."*

John Wain, *The Living World of Shakespeare*, 1964

ACKNOWLEDGEMENTS

The following publications have proved invaluable as sources of factual information and critical insight:

Linda Bamber, *The Woman Reader in King Lear*, from the Signet Classic edition of *King Lear*, edited by Russell Fraser, NAL Penguin, 1986

Allan Bloom and Harry V. Jaffa, *Shakespeare's Politics*, Basic Books, 1964

Charles Boyce, *Shakespeare A to Z*, Roundtable Press, 1990

A. C. Bradley, *Shakespearean Tragedy*, Macmillan, 1904

David Daiches, *A Critical History of English Literature*, Secker and Warburg, 1960

Northrop Frye, *On Shakespeare*, Yale University Press, 1986

Germaine Greer, *Shakespeare*, from the *Past Masters* series, edited by Keith Thomas, Oxford University Press, 1986

Ted Hughes, *Shakespeare and the Goddess of Complete Being*, Faber and Faber, 1992

G. Wilson Knight, *The Wheel of Fire*, Oxford University Press, 1930

L. C. Knights, *King Lear and the Great Tragedies*, from *The Pelican Guide to English Literature*, edited by Boris Ford, Penguin, 1955

Jan Kott, *Shakespeare Our Contemporary*, Doubleday, 1965

Maynard Mack, *Everybody's Shakespeare*, University of Nebraska Press, 1993

C. W. R. D. Moseley, *Shakespeare's History Plays*, Penguin, 1988

Kenneth Muir, Introduction to the Arden edition of *King Lear*, Methuen, 1972

George Orwell, *Lear, Tolstoy, and the Fool*, Penguin, 1947

Anne Righter, *Shakespeare and the Idea of the Play*, Chatto & Windus, 1962

Gary Taylor, *Reinventing Shakespeare*, Hogarth Press, 1990

Peter Thomson, *Shakespeare's Professional Career*, Cambridge University Press, 1992

John Wain, *The Living World of Shakespeare: A Playgoer's Guide*, Macmillan, 1964

John Dover Wilson, *Life in Shakespeare's England*, Cambridge University Press, 1911

All quotations from *King Lear* are taken from the Arden Shakespeare.